The Nature Within Us

A Journey Through Love, Reason, and What Makes Us Human

Albert Alarcon Jr.

Freedom Lake Publishing

The Nature Within Us

© 2025 Albert Alarcon Jr.

First Edition, 2025

Published by Freedom Lake Publishing

Printed in the United States of America

ISBN: 978-1-970921-00-7

© Freedom Lake Publishing

For those of us like you who want the world to be a little better,
you're not alone in that wish.

We are not alone.

Table of Contents

Before We Start

Why write about love?
Sometimes we look around at all the selfishness, greed, and plain old nonsense in the world, and we can't help thinking—someone should write a book about love. Then we laugh, because who can tackle something that big? But maybe that's exactly why we should. Each of us, in our own way, has lived, experienced, and needed love. Why not start the conversation together?

Then, of course, I laughed and asked myself, "Who am I to write about love? I write kids' stories and fables. I'm not a scientist, a psychologist, or some spiritual leader."

But then I thought about it—everyone's an expert on love in their own way. We've all lived it, lost it, needed it. So why not me? With some honest reflection and research, I think I can make it work.

What This Book Tries to Do
Another reason I want to write this is that, honestly, there are so many so-called experts out there, but they're either not doing it right, or their message just isn't reaching people. My goal is to be as objective as possible,

but I know much of what I'll write will come from my own thoughts and experiences. And that's okay.

In the end, I feel like this book needs to exist. "And if one day someone builds on these ideas and writes an even better book about love, I'll be the first to celebrate it."

A Note to All Readers

Before we dive in, there's something I should probably mention. We've got to be clear about the kind of stuff we'll be talking about here. If I bring up a quote or a story from some religious leader, know—I'm not trying to convert anybody. That's not the goal. I want to share different ideas and ways of thinking.

If you don't follow any religion, that's totally fine. Just think of it like you would any other philosophy. And if you *are* religious, I hope you'll give the same courtesy if I mention a teacher or beliefs you don't really agree with. Let's not throw out a good idea just because of who said it. Instead, let's listen, think it over, and decide for ourselves if it makes sense.

On Stories, Faith, and Open Minds

There's a lot of love talked about in every faith around the world, and that's a big reason I'll be pulling from them. Leaving that out would be like cutting off one of my best sources. So, if something rubs you the wrong way, imagine it's your grandparents saying it—or maybe some wise old guy on a porch somewhere—and take it in that spirit. Let's try to leave any old baggage at the door.

And that brings up another point: does it really matter *who* said something, or even if they actually said it? What matters is that the idea exists—it came from somewhere, even if it's just from me. For example, when I was younger, I used to love this

John Lennon song called *"I Found Out."* There's a line in it I always thought went like this...

"Don't let them fool you with dope and cocaine.
No, it can't harm you to feel your own pain."

That line stuck with me for years: *"No, it can't harm you to feel your own pain."* I took it on as a philosophy for life. Whenever I was heartbroken, stressed, or just dealing with whatever pain came my way, I'd think, *"It can't harm you to feel your own pain."* Even though the song wasn't actually about that—it had nothing to do with drugs like the lyrics suggested—I used it to get through most of my challenging moments. Feeling pain is part of life, and this phrase helped me remember that.

Later, when I learned how to play the song, I realized I'd remembered it wrong. But did it matter? Not at all. It had become part of my philosophy, and it still is to this day. I share it here as I remember it, not necessarily as it actually is. Hopefully, by the time you finish this book, you'll have a few empowering ideas of your own to carry with you.

The Art of Remembering Stories

Also, a heads-up: some of the stories I tell might not be 100% accurate to the original author or source. That's okay. I tell them as I remember them—or as they serve the purpose I need. Stories might be shorter, longer, or a little embellished. I'll try to give credit when I know it, and you can always look up the real version if you want. After all, how many times have you heard the story of Cinderella? How often do retellings mention her stepsister cutting off her toes? Or Pinocchio killing Jiminy Cricket? Funny, but true—and clearly, storytellers love a little embellishment.

As you read, keep this in mind: the goal here isn't to be perfectly accurate. The goal is to explore ideas of love and compassion—and yes, that means I'll be using an artistic license whenever I need to.

Another reason I'm writing this book comes from a quote by Gandhi I've always loved: *"Be the change you wish to see in the world."* Or at least, I think Gandhi said that. Either way, it's stuck with me, and it's part of why I felt compelled to share these ideas.

So, take a breath with me. Let's leave certainty behind and travel with curiosity. The only thing we really need to start is a little honesty, a little heart, and the willingness to listen to each other, to ourselves, and to the quiet places where love still waits to be remembered.

1. The Nature Within Us

I want to take us on a journey—a journey to a place we all secretly hope to reach. Along the way, I hope we can open ourselves to both reason and the emotions that guide it. Together, we'll arrive at a place where these truths already live inside us, even if they've been buried under our own prejudices, the biases of others, and the constant distractions of everyday life. After all, isn't modern life mostly about keeping ourselves busy with trivial things, avoiding what we might not want to face?

So, let's hop on this bike and take a ride. Let's imagine it as a gentle slope, mostly gliding, letting these ideas wash over us like the wind on a calm day. It should be an easy, leisurely ride to a place we've been searching for all along—a place where we can finally just be.

Where Philosophy Meets Humanity

So, where do we begin? Long, long ago, in a land far away—or at least far away from where I live—there was a man named Mencius. Mencius was one of the great Confucian philosophers of ancient China. He believed that kindness and empathy were built into our nature, like springs ready to flow when uncovered. His contemporary, Xunzi, another Confucian thinker, disagreed—he saw human nature as inherently wild and selfish, something that needed to be shaped through discipline and ritual.

I, like many of you, probably do lean toward Mencius's view: that people are born good. If you're not sure yet, I hope by the end of this, you'll be convinced. Think about it—who does a baby *not* love? Children tend to love everyone and are genuinely happy to meet new people. It seems that being antisocial or distant is something we learn over time. Maybe it's not so simple, but at least that's how it appears.

Have you ever noticed that children don't need to be taught to care? They reach out instinctively—to share a toy, to comfort a crying friend, to laugh without a reason. Perhaps the real question isn't if we're born good, but how we forgot that in the first place.

Philosophy can sound lofty until we see it played out in ordinary life. Sometimes the simplest stories reveal more about human nature than any lecture or essay ever could.

Well, that brings me to a story by Leo Tolstoy. This is how I remember the tale.

Little Girls Wiser Than Men

Two young girls, Mary and Natasha, were walking home from church. Mary looked around at the puddles left from the morning rain and said, "Let's run in the puddles!" It was now sunny and pleasant, and the idea seemed fantastic.

Natasha hesitated. "No, Mama will be angry if I ruin my Sunday dress," she said. Ruining a dress, especially her best, would surely be unforgivable.

But Mary was persuasive. After a bit of coaxing, Natasha gave in with a chuckle. The girls lifted their dresses as high as they could and started splashing through the puddles. Soon, they were jumping, kicking, and laughing, completely caught up in the fun.

Then it happened—Mary splashed mud all over Natasha's dress. Looking down, Natasha realized her shoes and stockings were muddy too. Her mother would definitely not be happy.

"Look what you've done to my dress!" Natasha shouted. Mary just giggled. That was the last straw for Natasha—she retaliated by pulling Mary's hair. Mary screamed in pain, loud enough to draw the attention of nearby adults, including both girls' parents.

The adults rushed over and immediately started arguing, each blaming the other for what had happened. The shouting escalated—all the adults began to shove, grab, and nearly came to blows. It was a mess.

Then someone asked, "Where are the girls?"

By the time the adults looked, Mary and Natasha had wandered off to another puddle. They had completely forgotten about the mud, the argument, and even each other's squabble. Now they were throwing sticks into the water, laughing and playing as though nothing had ever happened, completely unaware of the chaos behind them.

An onlooker shook their head and said, "Ah! Little girls are wiser than men."

Returning to Innocence

Well, that's how I remember this story anyway. I'm sure the real story was much longer, but hopefully the meaning isn't lost on us. Maybe the point isn't just to avoid pulling someone's hair when you're mad. Perhaps it's about being quick to forgive, or not starting a fight over something that didn't even happen to us, or that the people it did happen to don't even care about. Maybe it's about playing with someone who once wronged you. The possibilities are endless.

For our purposes, the takeaway is simple: children don't hold grudges. They haven't learned how yet. They forgive, they return to play, and they leave hurt behind them as lightly as footprints in rain. Perhaps that's the lesson hidden in their small forgiveness — a reminder of how soft the world can be before we learn to carry our wounds like armor. So let's begin our journey of love where they left off, trusting that people are born good, and that whatever truth we choose to carry becomes the path beneath our feet.

2. The Chemistry of Compassion

Many wise people have said, "The meaning of life is to love and be loved." That sounds poetic, but to me it's also practical. If we're born with the ability to love and be loved, it follows that we are born good—or at the very least, born *aimed* at goodness. And we don't have to believe that just because someone wiser said it. There's more to it than that. There's a science to it, and a simple, everyday experience we've probably felt a thousand times without naming it.

Imagine this: you're sitting at home alone, spouse or partner gone for the night. You're feeling kind of blue. Then the dog comes and sits at your feet, or the cat rubs against your leg and purrs. For a moment—just a moment—the blues lift. You feel better. Not as much as if your loved one were there, but still… better. That tiny warm spark in your chest? That's oxytocin. The love hormone. Built in. Part of your makeup from day one.

Our bodies produce hormones that influence our emotions and growth. When we feel these beautiful moments of connection, it's part of who we are. We are born this way—with the capacity to love and to be loved.

Here's another example. Let's picture ourselves stuck at a slow toll booth. We've been inching forward for what feels like forever, getting a little aggravated, maybe even muttering under our breath. But when we finally reach the booth, something in us shifts. We decide to pay our toll—and the toll for the next ten cars behind us.

Sure, we're now a little shorter on cash. But for some reason, we feel pretty good. That warm, lifted feeling isn't magic—it's serotonin. One of the "happy hormones." Our body's way of rewarding us for helping the group, contributing to the whole, or just doing something generous when we didn't have to.

And serotonin isn't alone. Endorphins, dopamine, oxytocin—they each have their part to play. Unless someone is born with a hormone deficiency, we're all built the same way: wired for connection, wired for kindness, wired to feel good when we make someone else's day better. In short, we were born to love and be loved.

Here's another story—this one from my own life—but I'm sure you've had a similar experience.

Kiss the Girl

When I was a boy, I walked a girl home from school—not my girlfriend yet, but I was hoping. I was goofing around, showing off the way kids do. Then, as we walked down that long path, our hands bumped—maybe hers bumped mine, maybe mine hers—and *bam*. Suddenly, we were holding hands.

I had never held a girl's hand before. Sure, adults made us hold hands crossing the street, but never like this—with a girl I liked. *Hubba hubba.* What a rush. My whole body felt tingly. Those were the endorphins— another hormone—along with the oxytocin.

We walked for what felt like forever. Maybe it was the endorphins, maybe dopamine, maybe just nerves, but I started thinking:

"Al, you should kiss her."
"Remember—don't get too close to her house."
"You don't want anyone to see."
"Especially not her mom or dad."

Then I turned and kissed her—just a little peck on the lips. But *whoa*. There was so much happening in that tiny moment. Oxytocin, because we were touching. Serotonin, because surely she was my girlfriend now. Endorphins, from all the excitement. And dopamine, because I actually did it—I kissed the girl.

I'm not a biologist, so I can't tell you the exact science of it, but this is the basic idea. Yes, putting love into hormones doesn't sound very poetic—but to me, it is. These chemicals allow us to feel these magnificent emotions. Of course, scientists will tell us love is far more complex than a handful of molecules—no single chemical explains a hug or a heartbreak. But sometimes a little poetry in the biology helps us see what the data alone can't:
Our bodies were built to care.

The point is simple: we are born good, with the ability to love and to be loved.

Circles That Expand
Now imagine a world where we really knew our neighbors. A world where we cared for them, and they cared for us. The truth is, we already live in that world —

we're just too indifferent to notice. We walk past the people in our own circle without seeing them, and they do the same with us.

Saint Teresa of Calcutta — Mother Teresa — once said, "If you want world peace, go home and love your family." To paraphrase her Nobel speech: love starts at home, then moves to our neighbors, then our country, and eventually the whole world. It's simple in theory: start with the people closest to us. Let our circle grow, touch other circles, and imagine a world where kindness spreads from one small group to another.

But let's be honest — that picture-perfect world where everyone holds hands and sings?
Yeah… that's not going to happen.
Not unless we're actually *born with the ability to love and be loved.*

And that's the point.
Whether through stories, science, or spirit, the pattern keeps whispering the same thing: *we were made for connection.*

This idea isn't new. Philosopher Peter Singer calls it the "expanding circle." Kindness that begins in the home can widen to include neighbors, strangers, and even all living things. Whether or not we've read his whole book, the core idea is something we already know: our love can grow larger than we think.

By now, we've reasoned together that love is natural — something we're born with.
Now it's time to speak to the heart.

Do you see yourself as a leader? Good leaders lead by example, and if we want a better world, we have to do our part. If we live with love, others are more likely to follow. Just as hairstyles change over time, so do attitudes.

So, whenever someone we know is struggling, don't avoid them. Take a moment to listen, even if we can't fix anything. And if you genuinely don't have the time, even a kind word —a simple hello —can make a difference.

The Weight of Indifference

You may have heard that the opposite of love isn't hate — it's indifference. And the more we think about it, the more it rings true. Hate still acknowledges someone. Indifference erases them. Ignoring someone is worse than disliking them. We can't help everyone, but we can help *someone*.

That reminds me of a fable you may already know:

Sand Dollars

A man was walking along a beach, picking up sand dollars and starfish and tossing them back into the sea. Another man approached and asked, "What are you doing?"
"I'm saving their lives," the first man said.
"But there are too many! You'll never save them all."
The man picked up another starfish, threw it into the water, and said, "I saved that one."

That's how life works. Every once in a while, we cross paths with someone who needs help — a friend, a family member, a neighbor, or even a stranger. If we believe in God, maybe we think God put them in our path. If we

13

don't believe in God, then maybe it was chance. Either way, we still have a responsibility as fellow human beings.

In Hawaii, people sometimes call strangers "cousin." I've always liked that. If all our ancestors came from Africa, then we really are one big family. Helping someone becomes easier when we see them as a cousin — someone who belongs to us.

Let's return to that idea: the opposite of love isn't hate — it's indifference.

Think of someone who needs help. Now, imagine we choose not to help. Not only that, but we respond with anger — maybe they're jobless, struggling, or making choices we don't understand. We say, "If you think we're going to help you, think again! Get off your butt! Do something, you loser!"

Of course, anger isn't kindness. It's not a gentle word or a helpful hand. But strangely, it's still better than being ignored. At least anger acknowledges a person's existence. They can defend themselves. They can reflect. They can grow. Above all, they are treated as a human being — someone with dignity.

But indifference?
Indifference gives them nothing.
No defense.
No reflection.
No dignity.

It treats a person as if they aren't even worth noticing — like a bug on the street. And when we ignore someone completely, we make them feel even less than that. Not intentionally, of course. But the harm is real.

None of us reading this book wants to be hateful. But if hate is still engagement, why do we so often choose indifference? Maybe we think being hateful is rude. Maybe we grew up with, "If you have nothing nice to say, don't say anything at all." Maybe we assume silence is neutral.

But silence isn't neutral.
Silence can be cruel.
Silence can be the thing that breaks a person.

Plato once said that we cannot be taught anything — we can only be reminded of what we already know, or shown something familiar from a new angle. That's what we're doing here. This isn't math. It's the stuff we know in our hearts.

Here's one more example. Imagine coming home late. The person you live with — spouse, partner, or parent — gives you the silent treatment. No welcome. No smile. No acknowledgment. And imagine this goes on for weeks, even months. Wouldn't you feel like you no longer belonged? Wouldn't you start to act out just to be noticed?

That's the power of indifference. Before anyone can grow, be better, or feel connected, they need one essential thing: **dignity**. And we give others dignity simply by acknowledging them. Sometimes that's as small as a hello. Sometimes it's saying their name.

Small things restore dignity.
Small things can save a life.
Just like one starfish at a time.

The Heart of Love

As we've seen, love shows up in many forms. We've connected it with goodness, kindness, dignity — and we haven't even begun to touch the full measure of it. Love is a big word, an ambiguous word, and maybe that's exactly why it works. If we tried to pin it down too tightly, we might lose the very beauty we're trying to describe.

Most of us know this passage from St. Paul in Corinthians:

Love is patient.
Love is kind.
It is not jealous.
It is not pompous.
It is not inflated.
It is not rude.
It does not seek its own interest.
It is not quick-tempered.
It does not brood over injury.
It does not rejoice over wrongdoing but rejoices with truth.
It bears all things, believes all things, endures all things.
Love never fails.

It's lovely as it is, but in an older translation, it reads much differently:

Charity suffereth long and is kind.
Charity envieth not.
Charity vaunteth not itself, is not puffed up.
Doth not behave itself unseemly; seeketh not her own.
Is not easily provoked.
Thinketh no evil.
Rejoiceth not in iniquity, but rejoiceth in the truth.

Beareth all things, believeth all things, hopeth all things, endureth all things.
Charity never faileth.

See how different it feels?
When we use the word *love*, the poem opens up. When we use the word *charity*, it seems smaller, more limited. Some scholars argue the original word is *agape*, but that can feel too large, too pure — something almost unreachable. And if a thing feels unreachable, why try?

That's why *love* works so well here.
Its very vagueness is what allows it to hold so much.

Love stretches the poem outward into all the meanings we live by:

- Brotherhood never fails.

- Passion never fails.

- Sincerity never fails.

- Kindness never fails.

- Unconditional love never fails.

- And countless others…

The point is simple: *love fills the gaps.*
When we say "love never fails," all these ideas come with it.

And remember, indifference is worse than hate. That brings me to another story…

17

Darla's Operation

Not long ago, my lovely wife Darla—who is a disabled veteran—had knee surgery and stayed at a VA rehabilitation facility. To visit her, I had to sign in on a small sheet of paper by the door. Twenty or thirty name lines, that's all. I'd arrive in the morning and stay until night—twelve to sixteen hours a day.

It was Christmas season, so groups of five or ten carolers passed through the halls here and there, singing gently. Outside, everyone talked about "supporting our veterans," waving flags, and speaking loudly about patriotism. Inside, the truth looked different.

When I signed in, I was a quarter of the way down the page. But when I left at night, the guard often hadn't even turned the sheet over. Some days, I signed out on the same page I had used the day before, with the carolers.

Two or three hundred veterans in that facility.
Fewer than thirty visitors.
At Christmas.

That kind of silence tells a story no speech ever could.

Darla shared her room with a former drill sergeant. She wasn't there for physical therapy. She came every year simply to give her home caregiver a break. And she never had visitors. Not one.

This woman was a burden to the nurses, constantly complaining and requesting things. They simply avoided her. Her every call for assistance wasn't out of rudeness but driven by loneliness, using her only remaining voice. When you feel unseen, even a complaint becomes a way to affirm, "I am still here."

Outside the building, veterans gathered in loud smoking circles, talking with the tough bravado men use to keep their pain at arm's length. Flags waved. People talked about "doing more for our troops."

But inside…
Inside, it was quiet.
Too quiet.
A whole hallway of men who had given everything, now spending Christmas with no one coming through the door.
That's indifference — not cruelty, not hatred, just the slow forgetting of people who should never be forgotten.

As Darla and I walked the wing, we met generals, an astronaut, a former White House staffer, and countless wartime veterans. Their smiles were small, proud, and practiced. Underneath each one, you could feel the ache of being overlooked.

One man told me about his daughter — how proud he was of her, how independent she'd become. He smiled when he said it, but then his face fell just a little.
There's a thin line between raising independent children and raising children who learn to keep their distance.
Not out of malice… but out of habit.
Out of the same kind of quiet indifference that grows when life pulls families apart piece by piece.
That moment stayed with me, because you could see both love and loneliness fighting in his eyes.

Then came a moment I'll never forget.

A woman from a church group came down the hall with a cart of handmade blankets. When she reached

Darla, she paused and said, "Hold on... I have a special one for you." She reached beneath the pile and pulled out a blanket she had set aside.

Darla was overwhelmed. Tears. Quiet, full, honest emotion.
And watching her, I felt it too.
It was like someone opened a window in a room that had been suffocating.

Love flowed through that moment—simple, human, unexpected. We didn't know that woman, and she didn't know us. But she broke through months of quiet with one small act of kindness — the opposite of indifference.

And I guarantee you: she remembers that moment, just as we do.

We never know how powerful we are.
A small act—something made, something brought, something offered with kindness—can shatter indifference in an instant.

Visiting friends or family, joining groups that give gifts, or donating to charitable clubs—any of these acts are powerful. We don't always know the impact we can have.

I hope this story shows that people are born good, or at least capable of love. Indifference is never the answer. And when we love those around us, the circle expands.

The Mystery of Why
If we're born good — or at least born with the ability to love and be loved — then why isn't everyone loving? That's the million-dollar question.

Humans aren't simple creatures. Life isn't solved by a slogan, even though we sometimes pretend it is. Gandhi said, "Be the change you wish to see in the world," and as beautiful as that is, it doesn't explain everything. There are deeper reasons—motives, instincts, fears—that shape the way we behave.

One obvious influence is how we're raised: parents, environment, friends, neighborhoods. That whole nature vs. nurture debate never seems to go away. But before diving into nurture, I want to focus on the natural wiring we all start with.

We humans carry old instincts that were essential in the ancient world: fight-or-flight, threat detection, and protecting what's ours. They helped our ancestors survive. But in the modern world, those instincts sometimes work against us. We react from fear when we should respond with understanding. We retreat when we should reach out.

During my research, I came across a study by Mark Sheskin, Paul Bloom, and Karen Wynn titled *Anti-Equality in Young Children.*
They wanted to know whether children would:

- give more to a stranger than themselves

- split things evenly

- or take less *just to make sure the stranger didn't get more*

The results were surprising.
Young children often acted to limit what the stranger received — even when it meant taking less for themselves.

When I discussed this with my father, he insisted that kind of behavior must be learned. However, other research complicates that idea. As the children got older, they became more fair.

Another study — by Bloom, Wynn, and Valerie Kuhlmeier — showed babies choosing between a "helper" puppet and a "hinderer." The babies overwhelmingly preferred the helper. Even infants recognize something like fairness, or at least goodness.

So what do we make of this?

It seems we're born with both capacities:

- the ability to recognize goodness

- and the instinct to guard ourselves, even when it looks like spite

Call it survival. Call it self-protection. Call it immaturity.
But it's in us.

What's interesting is that as children grow, their sense of fairness grows too. Whether that comes from environment, experience, or the natural unfolding of the mind, I don't know. Probably all three. But children learn. They adjust. They begin to understand that fairness benefits everyone.

When I think about this, I remember something from my childhood. Back in the "ancient days," boxes were held together with metal staples. My job was to break them down, prying out the staples with a knife. My younger sister always followed me around—maybe idolizing me, maybe just curious.

You can guess what happened.

I poked her in the eye.

(It's ok, she's fine now.)

Dad took us for ice cream afterward — well, *he* took her.

No ice cream for me.

Later, Mom told my sister to share. She said that if the roles were reversed, I would've shared with her.

(Would I really?)

There's a lot wrapped up in a moment like that:

- fairness

- empathy

- consequences

- and the old question every parent asks: *"How would you feel if it happened to you?"*

That question stays relevant long after childhood ends, though we forget to ask it as adults.

The Grace That Remains

As we grow older, our awareness expands from a small circle of school friends to a world full of apathy. We see wars, betrayal, homelessness, addiction, and even murder. It becomes harder to pause and ask, *"How would you feel if it happened to you?"* Life pulls at us — work, bills, exhaustion — and compassion slips through the cracks. But even so, it's a question we shouldn't ever let go of.

There's an old saying, not heard much anymore: "By the grace of God, there go I."

It's true, even for nonbelievers. Where we were born, who our parents were, how we look, whether we face disability or privilege — none of it was our choice. We didn't earn our starting line. We were given it.

And remembering that simple truth softens us. It reminds us how easily another life could have been ours — and how much we owe one another because of it.

By the grace of God, there go I.

3. Loving Ourselves

So far, our ride down this gentle slope has been pretty relaxed, but the next part of our journey gets a little more personal. It's about loving ourselves.

We think we know this—but do we really? Often, we act like we understand something simply because we've heard it before. Yet if we can't love ourselves—with all our strengths, weaknesses, quirks, and grandeur—it's going to be hard to love anyone else. Think about it: if we can't look past our own flaws, how can we look past someone else's? It bears repeating: how can we forgive another if we can't forgive ourselves?

We share whatever lives in our hearts. As the saying goes, what's in our hearts comes out of our mouths. If we harbor bad feelings about ourselves, we'll see bad everywhere we go. I often tell Darla when we plan a trip, "Wherever we go, we'll always be there." Meaning that no matter the place, we carry our own perspective—and our own mood—with us. I also joke, "When people complain on vacation, it's not because the place is bad, it's because they brought their own grumpiness along."

That reminds me of a fable I included in one of my earlier books, *Freedom at the Lake*.

The Barking Dog

One spring morning, a flock of birds was drinking dew from the grass when a dog burst in barking — "Grr — Ruff! Ruff!" Birds scattered into the trees, hearts racing. The dog barked at a squirrel, then a cat, then back at the birds.

Later, he went to the pond for a drink. When he saw his reflection, he growled at that, too.
One bird sighed to another, "Look — he's even angry at himself."

So often, we're no different. We aim our frustration outward when what we're really seeing is a reflection of our own hurt. We think others are mad at us when it's our own anger echoing back. We assume people dislike us because we secretly dislike ourselves. The truth is, we rarely know what's in another person's mind. Most of the time, we're reacting to our own reflection — just like that barking dog.

The Freedom to Feel

Before we go further, we need to talk about a kind of freedom most people never think about. Not political freedom. Not physical freedom. Something quieter, but far more personal: the freedom to feel.

When I was younger, I read the idea that we can control our emotions. That was a shock. All my life, I'd been told, "You can't help how you feel." But there it was, in black and white, with examples to prove otherwise. And I've found it to be true, though not always that simple.

26

Some emotions—like anger, lust, or jealousy—are called passions, from the same root as the word passive, meaning "to suffer." That makes sense. When anger hits, your blood pressure rises, your jaw tightens, and your instincts fire before your mind can catch up. We don't choose that initial spark. But after it, we do have a choice.

If we pause—even for a breath—we create space. And in that space, we can reframe. We can respond with intention instead of impulse.

Humans tend to live in two modes: will or whim.

People who live by will aim at something, make choices, and act to bring that aim to life.
People who live by whim drift along: "We'll cross that bridge when we get to it." "Go with the flow." "If it comes, it comes."

Not trying is the default. Trying takes effort. But the freedom remains—in every moment—to choose.

Early in the 20th century, the philosopher Jean-Paul Sartre said something dramatic but true: "Man is condemned to be free." At every turn, we have choices—how we feel, how we think, how we respond—and we live with the results. Pretending we have no choice, Sartre said, is living in bad faith. Lying to ourselves.

Growing up in San Francisco near the end of the flower-child movement, I met plenty of people with names like Butterfly and Ebony. Most didn't live long, but some of their wisdom stayed with me. Here's one story I still hold close:

Buddha and the Angry Man

Once, while Buddha was walking through a town, an angry man confronted him—shouting, accusing, and hurling insults as a crowd gathered. Buddha didn't argue. He simply nodded and walked on.

A man from the crowd followed and asked, "Why didn't you defend yourself? Why did you let him speak to you like that?"

Buddha replied, "If I give you a gift and you refuse it, who does it belong to?"

The man thought for a moment. "I suppose it still belongs to you," he said.

Buddha nodded. "It is the same with insults."

That story captures the main point: the initial feeling may not be your choice. Everything afterward is. Buddha chose, but we all have the same freedom—to notice the second feeling, to select the interpretation, to decide whether to carry the insult or leave it where it fell.

That is the freedom to feel.

Buddha lived by will, not whim. He chose his response. Few of us have his discipline, but the choice is always there. When we fail to choose, we react from whim—we get hurt, lash out, or carry anger we never needed to hold. But as Sartre said, we are condemned to be free. We live with the choices we make, whether they rise from will or whim.

And beneath all of this lies one simple truth: we are not slaves to our feelings. We may not control the first spark, but we can always choose what we do with the flame.

And that's really the heart of it: choosing how we respond, even when the first spark inside us wants to flare. Buddha showed it in his calm. We show it in smaller ways—places where our will and whim meet. And nothing reveals that better than what we learned as kids.

Remember when we were children and got caught doing something wrong? Our parents would ask why, and we'd shrug and say, "I don't know." Then came the corner, the timeout, the consequence. As adults, we don't stand in corners anymore—but life still gives us consequences, just in quieter ways. And that, too, is power.

Clearing a Space for Love

If our hearts are filled with love, there's simply no room left for anything else to take root. That's true for all of us. When love fills the space, resentment has nowhere to land, anger has nowhere to settle. Try filling your heart with love, and when bitterness comes around, it will find no vacancy.

That reminds me of another story.

The Zen Story
There once was a man who had studied for a long time. After many years of learning, he looked for the best teacher he could find. When he met him, he was eager to share everything he knew.

"I can teach you," the master said, "but first, we must have some tea."

They sat together, and the teacher poured. When the cup was full, he kept pouring.

"Stop! You'll spill it!" the student said.

The teacher smiled. "Like this cup, I can only teach where there is room. Without room, the tea spills over and becomes useless."

It's a simple image, but powerful. To learn, we must make space. To love, we must make room. If our hearts are overflowing with anger, fear, or resentment, where would love ever live? Sometimes, the first step toward loving others is clearing out what is weighing on us.

We've probably noticed this in our own lives: when we are lost in our feelings, and someone is trying to be kind. Their warmth doesn't always feel welcome—it challenges whatever darkness is already within us.

Sometimes, we try to be kind, but the person we're talking to is being unreasonable, and the kindest thing we can do is step back, smile, and stay peaceful. We never truly know what's in someone's heart.

Why fight with them?

My father used to say, "Son, don't fight with people who act stupidly. They were raised that way—it's not their fault." He wasn't excusing anyone; he was reminding me not to be dragged into someone else's storm.

And my mother would add, "If you have nothing nice to say, don't say anything at all." Not every battle deserves our voice. Sometimes walking away—maybe with a small smile—is the wisest choice we can make.

The Dignity of Self-Love

Before we talk about how we treat others, we need to look inward. Loving ourselves isn't arrogance — it's the foundation for everything that comes next.

Loving ourselves isn't vanity; it's dignity. It's the quiet way we treat the person we live with every day: our own heart. Just as we forgive our children or spouse when they stumble, we must learn to forgive ourselves. Emerson once wrote, "Speak what you think today in hard words, and tomorrow speak what tomorrow thinks, though it contradicts everything you said today." He wasn't praising contradictions — he was reminding us that we are meant to grow. Change is not hypocrisy. It's humanity.

When we were babies, we couldn't even hold our heads upright. No one holds that against us now. We've learned so much since then — and we're still learning. (If you picture me wobbling like a baby with a pencil in my hand, go ahead and smile. I am too.)

Being who we are, fully and honestly, is what makes life beautiful. Short, tall, young, old — so what? We don't need sameness. We need sincerity.

The Magic of Words

A lack of self-love can quietly turn into self-hate, and often it begins with the words we speak inside our own minds. When we say, "I'm stupid," or "I'm worthless," we're talking to the person we know better than anyone else. Would we ever say something like that to someone we love? Then why aim those words at ourselves?

In the Torah, "I Am" is God's name, and we're told not to take that name in vain. When we declare "I am" followed by something cruel — "I am nothing," "I am weak," "I am unworthy" — aren't we taking our own name in vain? The Toltec people taught that words are magic, that they cast spells over our minds. Whether or not you believe in literal magic, the principle holds: the words we repeat shape the world we walk through.

When we change our words, we change our lives. Gentle words soften the ground within us. Harsh words poison it. So let's speak to ourselves in a way that makes room for love rather than shutting it out.

Being ourselves can create tension when we crave acceptance. But we have to ask: whose acceptance are we chasing, and why? Is it from people who truly love us? Or from those who haven't yet learned to love themselves? These are hard questions, but important ones.

Advice for My Niece

One summer, my teenage niece was visiting from out of state. At a family gathering, she chose to sit with her grandmother and me while the other teens laughed outside. I smiled — it takes courage to sit with the old folks.

So I offered her something I wish someone had told me at her age:
Forgive yourself as you would forgive anyone else.
Carry yourself with dignity.
Love yourself, and you will be able to love others.
Remember, you can always choose your actions and your

responses.

You are free.

Buddha and the Angry Man (Conclusion)

After Buddha left the town where the angry man had shouted at him, the man followed to apologize.

"Don't you remember me?" the man asked. "I was the one who yelled at you."

Buddha smiled gently. "There's no need to apologize," he said, "for I do not see that man here today.

The lesson here mirrors the advice to my niece—and the heart of this chapter: we can choose how we respond, how we perceive, and how we live. Holding on to anger or regret is optional; forgiveness and love are within our reach.

When Love Begins Within

And as we continue down this road together, learning to forgive ourselves as easily as we forgive others, we begin to feel something lighter—a joy that sneaks up on us, like sunlight breaking through clouds. Because when love begins within, it naturally spreads outward. And when it spreads outward, we find we are no longer walking alone.

And that's where we can pause for a moment—right here, together. We've traveled through ideas both ancient and new, stories borrowed and stories lived, all leading us toward one simple truth: that love isn't something we have to chase. It's already within us, waiting to be remembered. We were born with it, though fear, noise, and distraction sometimes hide it away.

But each time we choose kindness over indifference, patience over frustration, compassion over judgment, we uncover that goodness again. And with it comes a quiet kind of joy—the kind that makes us smile without even realizing it. Because joy is what love feels like when it's shared. It's the warmth that rises when we recognize ourselves in someone else, when we see a spark of good and decide to nurture it.

We begin to see the thread that connects us—to our families, to our neighbors, and even to strangers who, in truth, are not strangers at all. This journey isn't about becoming something new; it's about returning to who we truly are—and finding happiness in that rediscovery.

So, as we move forward, let's keep choosing love and joy, even in small ways. Let's keep our hearts open to one another, our eyes kind, and our laughter close at hand. Because when we walk together with warmth and good humor, the world softens around us. And one day, we may realize the place we've been hoping to find was never far away—it's right here, in the simple joy of how we care for one another.

4. The Strength to Be Gentle

There's a line in *Sand and Foam* by one of my favorite writers, Kahlil Gibran:

"I use hate as a weapon to defend myself; had I been strong, I would never have needed that kind of weapon."

That sentence has followed me most of my life. It sits in my mind like a smooth river stone—small, simple, impossible to forget. Every so often, I pick it up again and turn it over in my thoughts. Gibran had a way of writing that keeps working on you long after the page is closed.

We live in a world that often mistakes kindness for weakness. Compassion is called "soft." People admire the ones who shout the loudest or hold their ground the hardest. But the older I get, the more I see that gentleness requires the greatest strength of all.
Anger and pride are easy—they flare up like sparks.
Love and patience are the fires you have to tend.

It takes strong will, care, and time.

I once saw a nurse smooth a blanket over a dying patient's hand and whisper a joke only he could hear. No medals, no applause—just quiet strength. That's gentleness at work.

That's true strength—the kind that doesn't boast, the kind that moves quietly through the world and still makes everything around it a little better.

What Honor Really Means

When Darla and I first got our apartment, we didn't even own a television. Nights were quiet—just conversation, the hum of the refrigerator, and whatever paperback I was chewing through at the time. One of those books was *The Black Cauldron* by Lloyd Alexander. I couldn't retell the plot today, but I remember the feeling it left behind: I kept circling around the idea of *honor*.

The story showed how differently people see it. For one person, honor meant courage; for another, sacrifice; for someone else, pride. And for a warrior, it might even mean killing bravely in battle.

That one stopped me cold. How could taking a life ever be honorable?
And yet, to the warrior, it was the ultimate act of loyalty or duty.

That contradiction stayed with me. I remember closing the book and sitting there in the quiet, thinking about it—both puzzled and humbled.

It made me realize how slippery the word really is— how one person's virtue can be another's sin, depending on the story they're in. Maybe honor isn't about *what* we do, but *why* we do it. The heart behind the action tells the truth.

After a lot of thinking—and more walking than I care to admit—the idea finally settled in me:

To live with honor is to live by our own values, especially when it's not easy.

That truth stayed with me. It wasn't something I figured out in a single flash—it grew on me, like a seed watered slowly over years. And when I thought about who taught me that kind of quiet strength, my mind went straight to my father.

He used to tell me, "A man is only as good as his word," and "Everyone loves a hard worker." He didn't need philosophy books; he handed me truths you could keep in your pocket. Those sayings became a compass— quiet, steady, always pointing in the right direction.

Honor doesn't shout. It doesn't need to.
It's that still voice inside that says, *Do the right thing, even if no one is watching.*
And the thing is—someone always is.

We are.

The Quiet Secret of Generosity

Regret is the lingering echo of overlooked honor. It settles in the chest like an old wound. But when we follow our inner compass, we avoid that kind of pain. The courage to stay kind, honest, and gentle—that's the quiet strength that keeps us whole.

Strength comes in many forms—physical, financial, emotional—but real strength always reveals itself through sharing.

We've all heard the saying, "Give till it hurts." I've always smiled at that and thought, *Maybe if giving hurts, we're giving from the wrong place.* When our love is full, giving feels light, not painful. It's joy, not duty.

And yet, it's often those who have the least who give the most. Ever notice that? People in need rarely stand outside the fancy stores—they go to the bargain shops and thrift stores. They know where compassion lives. The people who shop there may not have much, but they understand need, and that makes them more willing to give. Maybe that's the quiet secret of generosity: it grows strongest in those who remember what it feels like to need kindness.

Think about an older relative we love—someone who can turn even help into hard work. To love them well, we need patience, steady hands, and a calm mind. That's love with muscle.

If we don't have that kind of strength, we may suddenly find ourselves "too busy." That's human. But it's also a reminder that sharing love should feel uplifting, not draining. When we give from fullness, we grow stronger.

And that brings to mind a tale from *The Arabian Nights.*

The Man and the Witch – An Arabian Lesson

There once was a man who, unbeknownst to him, had married a witch. At first, she seemed like any other woman—devoted, graceful, maybe a bit mysterious. He thought he had been blessed.

But one evening, searching for his cloak, he found a small vial hidden in a chest, sealed with wax and carved with strange symbols. Curious, he broke the seal. The liquid shimmered like moonlight trapped in water.

When his wife returned home, he held up the vial.

"What is this?" he demanded.

Her face remained calm, but her eyes betrayed her. "Something you were not meant to find," she said softly.

Anger rose in him.
"Witchcraft!" he shouted. "You will stop this wickedness, or I'll have you cast out and punished."

This was in the old days—when men believed raising their voices made them strong, and women had few defenses but cunning. She bowed her head and said nothing. Inside, her fury sharpened like steel.

That night, she served him his favorite stew, seasoned with herbs—
and one drop from the vial.

He ate proudly. But when he stood, the room tilted. His words twisted into barks. His hands curled into paws. In horror, he realized he had become a dog.

He ran to her, pleading, but all she heard was barking.
She laughed, "You wanted to command me. Now go bark your orders elsewhere!"
She chased him from the house with a broom.

He bolted into the street, confused and hungry. Neighbors threw rocks. The butcher swung a stick when he scratched at the door. He fled again.

Eventually, hunger dragged him to a small bakery. Through the window, he watched the baker's daughter knead dough. She saw him—thin, frightened, tail low.

"Father," she said, "look at that poor thing. He's starving."

The baker waved her off.
"Be careful, child. Strays can be dangerous."

But the dog didn't growl or lunge. He simply sat, wagging once—as if to say, *I mean no harm.*

The girl's heart softened. She tossed him a bit of bread. He took it gently, and she noticed something strange—his eyes weren't wild. They were human. Full of sorrow, full of understanding.

That night, she left a bowl of milk outside. The dog returned and drank slowly, then curled near the door. The girl watched him, feeling something familiar rising—pity, yes, but also connection.

In time, she learned the truth from a wise woman who understood enchantments. Through a little courage, a little magic, and a lot of compassion, she reversed the spell.

When the man awoke, he wept—not from joy, but from shame.
"You saved me," he said. "Though I deserve nothing."

The girl smiled.
"Kindness costs nothing," she said. "But cruelty always collects its debt."

The proud man who once barked at the world had learned to speak softly.

Dignity in Kindness

That's the story as I remember it—or at least as I choose to tell it now. The details may have shifted over the years, but the lesson hasn't changed: when we push, demand, or force, we invite pain; when we soften and humble ourselves, we open the door to grace.

And that, I think, is what love does.
It teaches us to be strong enough to be gentle.

That story reminds me of another one I once wrote myself, in *Freedom at the Lake*.

There was an Osprey—a proud river hawk—who had ruled the sky. His wings cut through the air like blades, and trout flashed beneath him like quicksilver. But one day, while diving after a fish, he tangled his wing in a farmer's fence. He tore himself free, but the damage was done. From then on, he could glide only a short distance before dropping into the reeds.

He built his nest lower along the river, watching other Ospreys wheel overhead. Sometimes one of them would drop him a fish. If his pride was smaller than his hunger, he would eat it—but that wasn't often. Ospreys are proud birds.

An otter who lived nearby watched him for a while. The otter could see the truth: the Osprey wasn't arrogant; he was wounded. But otters know better than to offer pity openly—it only drives proud creatures deeper into their pain.

So the otter devised a plan.
He caught a fat, shining fish and laid it a few paces from

41

the Osprey's nest. Then he backed away, far enough to look like a threat, not a friend.

The Osprey screeched, puffed his feathers, and hobbled forward. The otter growled and splashed dramatically into the river, pretending to retreat. The Osprey struck the ground with his talons, seized the fish, and let out a triumphant cry that echoed along the bank.

From the water, the otter smiled.
He had found a way to feed the Osprey—and let him keep his dignity.

Sometimes kindness works best when it lets others keep their pride.

We've all met an Osprey or two—people who'd rather go hungry than accept help, not out of arrogance but because their dignity is stitched to their pride. And truth be told, we've all been that Osprey ourselves. It takes strength to offer help, but it takes a different strength to receive it.

When we let someone help us, we give them the chance to share, to be part of our story.
That isn't weakness—it's trust.

Standing Without Striking Back
And that brings me to a different kind of strength—the kind that stands without striking back.

When I was a boy, the civil rights movement was everywhere. What stayed with me wasn't the politics or the speeches—it was the faces. Determined. Tired. Brave. I remember the marches: people standing shoulder to shoulder with nothing but faith and stubborn hope to carry them forward.

One of those people was John Lewis.

He wasn't the biggest or the loudest, but he carried a strength that didn't bend. He marched across the Edmund Pettus Bridge in Selma, Alabama, knowing exactly what waited on the other side. The police stood ready with clubs and gas—prepared to make their point with pain. Lewis didn't meet them with fists or fury. He met them with resolve.

When the officers charged, he didn't run.
He stood his ground.
And they struck him down.

His skull was fractured.
But his spirit didn't crack.

The world saw a man beaten, but history remembers something far different.

Because strength doesn't always look the way we were taught.
Strength doesn't roar.
It doesn't dominate.
It doesn't demand to be feared.

Sometimes, strength is the person who stays standing when the world expects them to fall.
Sometimes, strength is the person who refuses to hate back.

Years later, that same officer asked to meet John Lewis. The two men sat together—older now, gentler, carrying years of reflection between them. The officer apologized. Lewis forgave him.

But let me ask you this:

When was that man stronger—
When he raised his club in anger,
Or when he reached out his hand in apology?

Humility like that takes courage. Forgiveness takes courage. Restraint takes courage. The quiet kind—the kind the world rarely celebrates, but desperately needs.

The Power of Humility

My father used to say, "The biggest man in the room is the one who doesn't have to prove it."
I didn't understand that when I was young. Back then, I thought strength meant volume, muscle, or being the one who gets the last word.

But as the years have passed, I see what he meant.
The people who carry love like armor rarely need to raise their voice.
They don't need to win the room; they just need to stay true.

And apologies—real apologies—take strength.
They strip us down.
They force us to step out from behind the shields we usually carry: pride, defensiveness, and excuses. When we apologize, we take off that armor and say to the world, "I am trusting you not to crush me for being honest."

What could be stronger than that?

Humility isn't weakness.
Humility is mastery.
Humility says, *I know who I am without having to show it to you.*

And maybe that's what all of this has been leading to:

Gentleness isn't the opposite of strength.
Gentleness is strength in its most mature form.

Because love—real love—doesn't avoid vulnerability. It walks straight into it.

Love asks us to keep our hearts open, even after they've been bruised.
It asks us to trust that the world can heal, even after it's shown us its worst.
It asks us to offer kindness, not because someone deserves it, but because *we've grown strong enough to give it freely.*

That's the strength John Lewis carried.
And it's the strength we're learning to carry together on this journey—
step by quiet step,
heart by steady heart.

Living the Lesson
We are strongest when we share what we have.
We are at peace when we make room for others' dignity.
And we are most human when we choose compassion over pride.

So let's keep going together—strong in love, steady in grace.
Let's be the ones who reach out instead of striking back,

who lift instead of lecture,
who speak softly but with hearts so full they echo.

If we can do that—if we can be that—then we won't
just be learning about love.
We'll be living it.

And maybe that's the quiet truth beneath every story
in this chapter.
From the witch's curse to the wounded Osprey, from the
marches in Selma to the simple act of accepting help:

Strength isn't in dominance.
Strength is in self-mastery.
Strength is in gentleness.

When we live that out—patiently, steadily,
imperfectly—we become the kind of people who leave
tenderness in our wake.
We become people who show others what is possible.
And we become people who, without even noticing, start
making the world around us a little easier to breathe in.

That is the strength to be gentle.
And it is ours to carry, step by quiet step,
wherever this journey of love takes us next.

5. The Road of Power

We've been coasting downhill for a while now, letting the ideas of love and gentleness carry us along. But every easy ride eventually meets a climb, and this next stretch is uphill. It's where we start to talk about *power*—how it tempts us, how it changes us, and how it can pull us away from love if we're not careful.

So, shift your weight a little, breathe steady, and pedal with me. This is where the real work begins.

Power isn't evil on its own. It's like wind—it can lift us or knock us over. In the right hands, it builds cities, saves lives, comforts the lost. In the wrong hands, it bruises hearts and silences voices. Every one of us carries some form of it, even if we don't always recognize it. Some use words as their power, some use silence, some use position or wealth. The danger isn't in having power—it's in forgetting what it's for.

True power should serve, not control. It should raise others, not press them down. But the line between leading and ruling can be so thin that we often cross it without noticing. A little pride here, a little fear there—and before we know it, we're not guiding, we're gripping.

We've all seen it happen. Maybe we've done it ourselves—using our authority, our experience, or even our hurt to win an argument or to make someone small. At the time, it can feel good, even justified. But afterward, if we're honest, it leaves a taste that isn't joy. It's emptiness dressed as victory.

That's the strange thing about power: when we use it to feel big, it only reminds us how small we still feel inside. Real strength, as we've seen, comes from love. It builds rather than breaks.

I've never been much of a Nietzsche fan. Reading him feels like walking through a storm—lightning flashes of brilliance followed by thunder that shakes your peace. Still, he gave us ideas worth wrestling with, and *the Will to Power* is one of them. He believed that at the heart of all human behavior lies one driving force—the will to grow stronger, to assert, to master. In his view, it was the pulse behind ambition, creation, and even survival.

It's not a bad theory, at least on the surface. But sometimes, in chasing strength, we forget that love is the only power that doesn't consume us in the process.

And that brings us to a story—a familiar one, told many times before, about a man who wanted to feel strong and ended up becoming something else entirely.

The Ambition of Gary

It was graduation day. Gary finished near the top of his class in chemistry and biology, but not quite enough to stand out. There were no major awards with his name on them; only awards that mentioned him were among the many talented science students. No speeches, no spotlight. Gary sat through the ceremony listening to others—some, he thought, of lesser intellect—receive the praise he believed was meant for him.

As a boy, Gary had been small and quiet, the kind of child who spent recess watching from the edges. His parents would tell him, "One day they'll move out of your way, Gary." But even as an adult, they never did.

When he became a research scientist, he found himself an overachiever among overachievers once again. Worse still, his bosses weren't scientists at all—they were finance people, "money types" who spoke in trends and margins instead of formulas and ideas. His accomplishments were often overlooked in the race for what was "new."

Then came the idea that changed everything. Gary wondered if evolution could be reversed.
What if we could reawaken the ancient instincts buried deep within us—the primal confidence, the dominance, the fearlessness?

Through a strange mix of genius and desperation, he found a way.

Gary tested the treatment on himself. At first, it felt like everything he'd ever wanted. He stood taller, spoke louder, and people paid attention. For the first time, Gary felt powerful.

But power without restraint doesn't steady—it accelerates.
Soon, he became irritable and aggressive. When things didn't go his way, he lashed out. His colleagues walked on eggshells. His friend Tom, a kind man who often mediated Gary's conflicts, tried to talk with him. Rita—

bright, steady, compassionate—became a target of both Gary's admiration and resentment.

One night, after drinks, Gary's envy boiled over into violence. Tom stepped between him and Rita, trying to calm him down. Gary saw it as another man taking what he believed was his. Rage flooded him—fast, hot, unthinking.

He hit Tom.
Then he kept hitting.

When it was done, he dragged Tom's body into the bushes and left him there.

Rita was waiting—worried, unaware. Gary smiled softly, voice gentle.
"Everything's all right. You'll understand soon."

He gave her the treatment. He wanted her to become like him—strong, ruthless, reshaped.

And that's what power does when it loses love: it stops admiring and starts molding.
It says, *Be like me... or you're less.*

The Nature of Power

We are not wolves.

We may carry their instincts—the hunger, the drive, the need to protect what's ours—but we were never meant to live by tooth and claw alone. The strength that built our world didn't come from domination; it came from cooperation. We survived not because we were the strongest, but because we were the only ones who could imagine a better way to live *together*.

When danger came, we gathered around the fire. When the hunt failed, we shared what little we had. When the night felt too long, we told stories to remind each other that dawn always comes. That's how civilization began—not with the biggest club, but with the first outstretched hand.

Gary forgot that. He let his will to power devour the part of himself that could still feel compassion. Once power becomes hunger, it's never satisfied—it feeds on itself until nothing's left but instinct.

Can we imagine that moment?
Someone we care for—someone we once saw as an equal—suddenly turning us into a project, something to mold? How would that feel? How many times in smaller ways have we done the same—demanding others think like us, love like us, react like us?

Gary's story isn't just about him. It's about all of us when we forget that love requires difference. It asks for balance, not mirrors.

Because when we begin forcing others to become us, we both vanish.

The Pendulum of Power

Somewhere along the way, we began to confuse dominance with confidence. We reward the ones who shout the loudest and mistake volume for vision. Words like *alpha* and *winner* became badges, as though life were a contest and empathy a weakness.

But we aren't packs fighting for hierarchy. We're communities trying to stay human.

Right now, it feels like we're swinging toward hardness again—sarcasm, detachment, indifference. People scroll past suffering, shrug at cruelty, laugh at outrage. We call it realism, but it's really fatigue. *Compassion takes energy, and many of us are worn thin. But fatigue doesn't erase responsibility — it just tempts us to forget it.*

That's the thing about pendulums—they don't stay on one side forever. They always swing back. And maybe that's where we come in.

Every time we choose to listen instead of shout, to build instead of break, to forgive instead of prove right— we pull that weight toward center.

Maybe the real will to power isn't control over others, but mastery of self.
The power to stay kind in an unkind moment.
The power to walk away instead of striking back.
The power to see through the noise and keep our balance.

We can do that. We already are.

The Road That Teaches Us
Maybe that's what this whole ride has been about— not reaching some grand destination, but remembering how much strength we already carry in our hearts. Real power was never about control. It was never about being louder, or tougher, or first in line. It was about gentleness in motion—the steady hand, the patient ear, the soft word that can stop a storm before it starts.

We don't have to change the whole world to change the way the world feels.

We just have to keep showing up—with kindness, with courage, with love that refuses to stay quiet.

Love isn't something we perform in perfect conditions. It's what shows up when conditions aren't perfect—when the day goes sideways, when someone cuts us off in traffic, when burnt toast starts the morning. That's where love gains its muscle. Those small choices, those quiet kindnesses, are the real training ground.

So let's keep pedaling together, even up the hard hills. Every act of patience, every moment we forgive, every kindness we offer—it all adds up. And one day, when we look back, we'll realize we weren't just learning about love or strength at all.

We were becoming both—one deep breath, one soft word, one steady climb at a time.

6. Seeing the Worth in Others

Maybe this is where we pull over for a bit, let the engine cool, and take a look at where we've been. Up to now, we've talked about love, self-respect, and what it means to hold our values steady. But every road eventually leads to this question:

How do we treat others when there's nothing in it for us?

I came across this story only recently, though it feels like something I should've known all along. I remember telling Darla about it because it says something about how we see others' worth.

My Retelling of Jack London's The Heathen

They say men reveal themselves in storms—and that's how I met Otoo.

It was during a South Pacific yacht race aboard the *Ariel*, a sleek schooner slicing through warm seas. But we never saw the hurricane coming. The sky turned to ash, the sea rose like a wall, and the *Ariel* shattered like glass. I clung to a piece of wreckage, nearly senseless, when a powerful hand grabbed hold of me.

Otoo.

A Kanaka sailor from the islands—strong, patient, quiet. He never said much. He just held on.

For days we drifted—sunburnt, starving, water rationed to mouthfuls. He gave me his portion more than once. He was resourceful, steady, and asked for nothing.

When a trader's schooner finally spotted us and pulled us aboard, I tried to pay him. Gold, trinkets, anything. I even offered to make him my servant. But he looked at me calmly and said,
"I'm not your servant. We are brothers."

And so we were.

From then on, in every venture—every shady port, every dangerous deal—I was the face, and he was the shadow at my back. Never asked, never wavered. Just stood beside me. My brother. My protector. My friend.

They called him a heathen. Said he'd never seen a Bible or heard a hymn. But I've never known a man more honest, more loyal, more brave.

People laughed sometimes—at us, at him. Said it wasn't proper. But Otoo didn't care. And after a while, neither did I.

And when the end came—one last time, in one final storm—Otoo saved me again. Gave his life so I could keep mine. I buried him myself beneath a breadfruit tree, on the island where we'd first washed ashore. On the stone, I carved the only words that ever truly fit:

Otoo, My Brother.

When we think about it, it's really a story about respect—about seeing another person not for what they can give us, but for who they are. Otoo, though different from Jack in nearly every way, showed what strength looks like without pride, what love looks like without pretense.

When I first read London's story, I sat for a while thinking about Otoo—the quiet way he lived his values. It reminded me that moral wisdom doesn't always arrive from sermons or books; sometimes it's handed to us in another person's courage.

Kant's Measure of Humanity

That idea shows up again and again in life, but one of the clearest voices to ever explain it was the philosopher Immanuel Kant. He wrote:

We should always treat humanity, whether in ourselves or in others, as an end and never merely as a means.

It may sound lofty, but it's simple in practice:
Don't use people.
Don't reduce them to what they can do for you.

We live in a world that measures people by usefulness—how efficient, marketable, or profitable they are. But dignity has no price tag. Otoo had nothing by the world's standards, and yet he was rich in the truest sense.

He didn't save Jack for a reward. He didn't weigh the cost. He acted from something deeper—a strength born from seeing another human as an equal, not as a tool.

When we look at life that way, the measure of everything changes. Success becomes less about what we gain and more about what we give. Power becomes less about control and more about compassion.

Maybe that's the quiet test of character—not how loudly we win, but how gently we stand beside others.

The World That Forgets

But sometimes we wake up and realize how easily the world forgets this. There's a modern idea people now call *hustle culture*. It tells us that every minute, every talent, every connection should be squeezed into something useful. It sounds like ambition, but more often, it turns people into products—and that's when we forget they're people at all.

The world may spin faster now, but kindness still walks at a human pace.

That's where Kant's old idea comes back around: treat humanity—our own or another's—as an end, never just a means. In simpler words:

Don't use people. They're not stepping-stones.

There's even a song by The Monkees that puts it plain:
"I'm Not Your Steppin' Stone."
If you don't know it, trust me—it still hits.

When we forget the worth of others, we trade connection for transaction.
When we remember, the world feels human again.

As we said earlier, indifference—treating others as if they don't matter—is the opposite of love. Otoo showed what it looks like to live the other way: to see worth before usefulness, to give without keeping score, to act from respect instead of self-interest.

It's something we can all practice in small ways—by noticing the invisible people, by offering patience where the world offers hurry, and by remembering that everyone we meet carries a whole story behind their eyes.

And when we start to live that way, we discover something quietly joyful:

We are never as separate as we think.
We are all brothers and sisters.

7. The Quiet Kind of Love

So maybe now's a good time to get back on the bike, feel the stretch of pavement beneath us, and look ahead at what's coming next: the quiet kind of love. Not the kind that makes speeches or headlines, but the kind that simply stays. The love that doesn't ask what someone can do for us, but how we can meet them where they are.

This road is softer—steady, gentle, and a little more personal. Because after learning to see the worth in others, the next step is learning how to hold that worth—with patience, kindness, and care.

Most love isn't dramatic anyway. It doesn't need to be. It's the love that gets up early, makes coffee, forgives without fanfare, and keeps showing up. It's the steady heartbeat of life—the quiet rhythm that makes the big moments possible.

And something happens when we stop chasing perfection. When we stop waiting for the movie version of love and start accepting what's real—the flaws, the wear, the cracks in people and in life. That's when something softer appears. Something lasting.

Because love was never meant to be flawless.
It was meant to be faithful.

And that brings us to a story.

The Broken Teacup

There was once a person who had a cup they used every morning. It wasn't anything special—just part of the ritual that made the day feel steady. Coffee, tea, a few quiet minutes before the world began shouting again. Then one morning, the cup slipped from their hands and broke clean in two.

That small cracking sound carried more meaning than it should have.
That's it, they thought. It's ruined.

But a craftsman offered to mend it using *kintsugi*, the Japanese art of repairing broken pottery with gold. When the cup returned, its cracks glowed softly—threads of gold tracing the places where life had once split it open. It was still a cup, still capable, but now it carried its story openly.

Then something interesting happened. When guests visited, the owner found themselves telling the story of the cup—how it broke, how it was repaired, how the cracks became the most beautiful part. They didn't hide the damage; they lifted it up. And each time they did, they smiled. Their guests did too.

The cup had become a quiet kind of teacher.

That's the spirit of **Wabi-Sabi**—the idea that beauty isn't found in perfection, but in acceptance. Weathered things, worn things, things softened by time—these hold a deeper grace than anything untouched.

And really, we've seen this lesson before.

Earlier, when we learned to forgive ourselves.
When we learned to let go of old shame.
When we learned that our dents and scratches don't
disqualify us from love, they prepare us for it.

Kintsugi is simply that lesson turned outward.

Compassion works the same way. People rarely come
to us flawless. They're chipped, tired, uncertain. They've
been dropped by life a few times. And yet, when we stop
trying to fix everyone and start honoring the cracks,
something shifts. We stop expecting perfection and start
appreciating the long road that shaped each person.

Love isn't about hiding the flaws.
It's about seeing the gold in them.

And maybe our purpose—the quiet one underneath
all our noise—is to be part of that gold. The shimmer that
helps someone else stay whole.

. When we start seeing the world this way—made of
cracks and gold—we realize something simple but
profound: **everyone carries a story.**
Every person we meet has been dropped by life a few
times. Some are still gathering their pieces; others wear
their repairs proudly.

Seeing that truth softens us.
We stop rushing to judge.
We start listening.

Because understanding someone doesn't mean we
agree with them—it just means we're standing close
enough to see what shaped them. And once we can see
what shaped them, compassion becomes almost instinct.

61

Behind anger, there's usually fear.
Behind pride, there's often loneliness.
Behind stubbornness, a fragile kind of hope.

When we look through another's eyes—even for a moment—the world begins to make sense again. The noise fades. The edges soften. What's left is understanding—not perfect, but enough—enough to talk without shouting, to forgive without forgetting, to care without demanding anything in return.

That's what love looks like when it's still and steady: *The willingness to see a person's cracks without making them feel broken.*

But love doesn't stay still forever.

Once compassion deepens, it eventually rises to its feet.
It moves.
It acts.

This brings us to the next part of the road—where love stops being a quiet feeling and becomes a living choice.

Love in Action

Compassion that never moves stays comfortable, but not useful. At some point, love has to leave the safety of our thoughts and step out into the world. That's when it stops being an idea and becomes a way of living.

The world often tells us to measure our worth by what we own—money, comfort, recognition. But love doesn't count that way. It doesn't keep score. It only asks,

Did we show up? Did we try to understand? Did we care when no one was watching?

And maybe to see what love looks like in motion, we need a story that's already shown millions of people what forgiveness looks like when it refuses to hesitate.

Most of us know the story of the prodigal son — a young man restless and full of dreams. He asked his father for his inheritance early, wanting to live on his own terms. The father, though heartbroken, gave it to him. Sometimes love means letting go, even when every part of you wants to hold on.

The son left in a rush of excitement. For a while, life was good — music, friends, laughter. But when the money ran out, so did the company. Hunger followed, and the glamour faded. He found work feeding pigs, forgotten and cold.

One day, staring at the husks the animals ate, he realized even his father's servants lived better than this. He didn't plan a speech; he just decided to go home and face whatever waited — even rejection. He practiced a few words along the road:
Father, I've done wrong. I don't deserve to be your son. Just let me work for you.

Most of us say we believe in forgiveness, but few of us are willing to be the first one to move. But before he even reached the house, his father saw him coming and ran to meet him.
He didn't wait for the apology.
He ran.

He threw his arms around his son and wept. No questions, no judgment—just love in motion. He called for food, for music, for a new robe. The son tried to speak his apology, but the father was already preparing a feast.

That's how real love works—it doesn't wait to be asked, and it doesn't wait for perfection. It moves first, and that's what makes it powerful. It moves. It heals through doing.

Outside, the older brother refused to join the celebration. He couldn't understand why his father would honor the one who failed. But the father said softly, "You are always with me, and everything I have is yours. But your brother was lost, and now he's found."

The father wasn't keeping score. He wasn't counting what was lost. He was celebrating what had been restored.

When we measure people by what they deserve, the heart closes. When we measure by what can still be restored, it opens.

And if we look closely, we can see the same gold that ran through the broken cup running through this story, too. The father didn't hide the cracks—he filled them. His forgiveness was the gold that made the family whole again.

The Journey Together

We all take turns playing both roles—the prodigal and the father.
We wander, we return.
We forgive, we are forgiven.

And along the way, we learn that love only becomes real when it *moves*.

When it forgives instead of holding grudges.
When it listens instead of lecturing.
When it opens its arms instead of crossing them.

Love in action changes everything. It changes homes, friendships, and even the way strangers stand side by side in line.

Sometimes, it's as simple as showing up when someone else expects no one will.
Other times, it's saying, "I forgive you," even when the hurt still aches.
And sometimes, it's just smiling at the cracks—in our lives, our people, and ourselves—and saying, "Look how far we've come."

Love asks very little of us, except this: don't stay still when someone needs you to move.

So maybe this little stop—this cup of something warm, this quiet stretch of road—wasn't about learning anything new at all. Maybe it was just about remembering that we've known this truth all along:

Love, in all its forms, is both the gold and the glue. It's the part that holds us together when the world tries to split us apart.

8. The Courage to Grow

There are times when love seems to shrink, not because it disappears, but because fear begins to crowd it. The more we guard ourselves, the smaller our hearts become. Love, when it's alive, wants room to move. It wants to reach and be reached. It wants to see the world not as a collection of strangers, but as a shared home.

When we let love expand, it changes the way we see. It reminds us that compassion and understanding aren't luxuries of the spirit; they are its daily work. The kind of work that often asks us to listen when we'd rather speak, to forgive when we have every reason not to, to see the person behind the behavior.

Let's admit it — we've all had days when kindness feels like too much to ask. Days when we do not snap at someone should earn us a medal. Ha Ha. But still, love asks us to try again — not because people always deserve it, but because *we* deserve the peace that comes from keeping our hearts open.

Every act of care expands us. Every time we resist bitterness, the world grows a little larger. And maybe that's the quiet secret: love doesn't change the world in an instant; it changes *us* first, one gentle act at a time.

The Work of Compassion

Compassion isn't theory; it's participation. It's what happens when we care enough to notice and stay long enough to help. It's the courage to show up for another person, even when it costs us a little of our comfort.

I recall a time in Sicily, in the town of Syracuse, when Darla and I were wandering the old market streets. We saw an elderly woman walking slowly along the cobblestones, her hands trembling. A shopkeeper noticed her, left his store unattended, crossed the street, and helped her find a seat. Then he bought her a small coffee from a nearby stall and told the vendor, "Put it on my tab — I'll pay you later." He stayed with her until she was steady again.

It wasn't a grand act. No applause. Just a quiet man who understood that caring for another soul was worth more than guarding his inventory. That moment has stayed with me ever since. It was the gospel of compassion written in the language of everyday life.

Let's admit it — it's not easy to live like that. Compassion asks us to move beyond convenience. It's not about fixing the whole world, only about refusing to ignore what's in front of us. It takes practice, patience, and sometimes, a little humor to keep trying.

The world can make us tired, but compassion renews us. Every act of kindness is a small defiance against despair. And if we keep choosing that defiance — in a shop, on a street, in a quiet conversation — the world might not change overnight, but it will notice.

The Discipline of Growth

Growth is one of those words that sounds gentle until it happens to us.

We all say we want to grow — and we mean it — but not in *this* way, not in the way that stretches us where we're sore or shines a light on what we'd rather not see. Growth sounds noble in books. In real life, it feels more like a pair of shoes one size too small.

It's not that we don't want to improve; we just want to do it without being uncomfortable. We want the wisdom, not the embarrassment that usually teaches it. We want patience, but preferably without anyone testing it.

Real growth, though, doesn't happen in comfort. It humbles us first. It holds up a mirror that we'd rather not look into. It shows us the things we still cling to, the stories we tell ourselves to stay the same.

As my father used to tell me, *"If you want to learn, you need to be humble."*
When we were children, growth was easier. We expected to fall, to scrape a knee, not to know. But now that we're grown — or at least supposed to be — we act like we're already supposed to have it figured out. Admitting we don't is somehow more complicated than the lesson itself.

That's what humility really is — the doorway to understanding. It's admitting that life still has something to teach us, even after all the lessons we thought we'd mastered.

We've all had our "bike" moments — insisting, "Dad, don't hold the seat!" until gravity reminds us that maybe we could use a little help. Then we dust ourselves off and say, "Okay, Dad… maybe hold it a little." Growth looks like that — pride giving way to trust, and a bit of laughter along the way.

When we stop learning, our care turns mechanical. We start choosing who deserves our kindness instead of asking what our kindness might do.

Growth, then, isn't about chasing perfection; it's about staying teachable. Every day brings another chance to loosen our grip, to see with softer eyes, to admit that we still have more to learn. It's not a contest, and it's not a straight line — it's a long conversation with life itself.

Each of us learns in our own way. Sometimes the lesson arrives wrapped in joy, sometimes in frustration. Either way, it asks the same question: *Will we stay open?*

Because growth, at its heart, is an act of courage — the willingness to let go of who we were for the sake of who we might become.

And that is where the next step begins.

The Courage to Change

Growth is the lesson; courage is what puts it into practice.

We all like the idea of change — just not the part where it actually happens. It's funny how often we pray for things to be different, then call them "problems" when they finally are.

Real change asks something of us. It wants honesty, and honesty has a way of rearranging the furniture. Suddenly, what once felt steady doesn't fit anymore. The old habits, the small defenses, the familiar excuses — they start creaking under the weight of what we've outgrown.

It's tempting to cling to what's known, even when it isn't working. We tell ourselves, *At least I understand this pain.* It's easier to stay in a tight space than risk the open one. But eventually, something inside whispers, *You can't keep living small.*

That's where courage begins — not in grand moments, but in quiet ones. The courage to admit something isn't right. The courage to listen instead of react. The courage to stop saying, "I'm fine," when we're not.

Courage rarely feels like courage in the moment. It feels like confusion, or fear, or walking through fog. We picture bravery as loud, but most of the time it's steady — a small step forward when we'd rather sit still.

There's an old story about two men from a small village who had been friends since boyhood. For years, they talked about making a great journey — a pilgrimage to Jerusalem. It became their shared dream, something they'd mention every planting season and every harvest. "Next year," one would say.
"Next year," the other would answer.
And somehow the years kept slipping by.

Finally, when they were both old and their hands were too stiff for much work, they decided it was now or never. They sold what little they had, kissed their families goodbye, and set out walking before sunrise. They agreed to be back by autumn — enough time, they thought, to make the long journey there and back again.

For the first few days, they walked side by side, light-hearted, talking like boys again. But not far into the journey, they came upon a small village struck by famine — families living in broken huts, children weak from hunger, mothers boiling weeds for soup.

One of the old men said, "We should stop and help." The other shook his head. "If we do, we'll lose too much time. Remember, brother — Jerusalem."

So, they parted ways.

The traveler who kept going pressed on through dust and heat, steady in his purpose. He reached Jerusalem just before autumn and stood where he had always dreamed of standing. He prayed, wept, and gave thanks for the journey that had been completed.

Meanwhile, his friend stayed behind. He fixed roofs with his calloused hands, shared what food he had, and taught the children how to plant small gardens. Weeks turned into months, and he never did leave.

When the traveler finally returned home, he went to visit his old friend. He found him thinner, slower, but surrounded by laughter — the same children now running in the fields he had helped plant.

"You never made it," the traveler said softly. His friend smiled. "I did, brother. I just found my Jerusalem sooner."

Sometimes courage isn't about reaching the goal we set out for — it's about recognizing the purpose that finds us along the way.

We picture courage as heroic, but often it's simply choosing compassion over completion, people over plans. It's realizing that the journey isn't measured by miles but by mercy.

Change often feels like loss until we live through it. Letting go rarely feels good in the moment, but somewhere on the other side of fear, peace waits patiently.

Life, of course, has a sense of humor. It keeps sending the same lessons in new packaging until we finally open them. Sometimes, the very people or problems we resist the most are the ones that carry us to our next step forward.

Courage isn't loud or flashy. It's quiet faith in motion — the choice to walk toward what's uncertain without demanding a guarantee. It's what allows the heart to breathe again after being closed too long.

We don't get to control when change comes, only how we meet it — with resistance, or with grace.
And maybe grace is just another word for walking forward, even when we don't yet see where the road bends.

Maybe the courage to change isn't found on the road ahead, but in the heart willing to stop along the way.

The Courage to Grow

As we look back, we have traced the quiet path of transformation — how love, compassion, and self-awareness shape the way we live with one another.

Love, at its best, widens our vision. It teaches us to see the worth in others and reminds us that connection is what gives life meaning. Compassion is not weakness; it's the strength that keeps humanity from hardening.

Growth follows in its gentle way — not the kind measured by success or achievement, but by humility, the willingness to stay teachable. It rarely feels noble while it's happening. It's awkward, unflattering, and sometimes exhausting. Yet through it we learn patience, humor, and gentleness — toward others and toward ourselves.

And courage — that quiet, steady force — is what makes all change possible. It rarely arrives with fanfare; it's the soft resolve to keep moving even while fear still lingers. The story of the two old friends on their long walk to Jerusalem reminds us that the truest pilgrimages aren't always the ones that reach their destination. Sometimes, compassion asks us to stop along the way — to trade completion for connection.

Taken together, these moments reveal a simple truth: Growth asks for humility, change requires courage, and both are guided by love.

Life doesn't move in straight lines. We stumble, learn, and begin again — sometimes with laughter, sometimes with a sigh. But if we can keep our hearts open, if we can stay teachable and brave enough to keep walking, we'll find that every road — even the detours — leads us closer to understanding.

Maybe that's all love asks of us in the end:
to keep growing, to keep changing,
And to meet each other kindly along the way.

9. Love Behind Walls

The road climbs again, a slow, steady rise that makes the legs ache, and the breath come shorter. We've been riding for a while now — through laughter, lessons, and quiet stretches of reflection — and this part asks a little more of us.

As the incline sharpens, we can almost hear our knees complain, feel the burn in our thighs, and the tightness in our chest. These climbs come to all of us sooner or later — when the years start to weigh heavier, when old injuries remind us they never fully left, when absence sits beside us at the table. And when those moments arrive, love doesn't vanish — it just has to travel uphill too.

That's where our next lesson begins.

There are days when the body reminds us it has limits.
The knees ache when we stand, the back protests when we bend, and even a short walk feels like a small act of courage. Sleep comes lightly, laughter takes effort, and sometimes, kindness itself feels like work.

When pain becomes constant, love can grow quiet. Not because it's gone, but because there's not much strength left to give it shape.

Pain builds walls around the heart—not to keep others out, but to protect what remains inside.

We don't always notice when it happens. The smile fades first, then the easy warmth in our voice.
The world doesn't seem unkind, just distant. Pain doesn't alter who we love — it changes what we have left to give.
And maybe that's where compassion begins — not in understanding pain, but in remembering how it can cause us to withdraw from the world.

Understanding the Needs Beneath Love

Years ago, a psychologist named Abraham Maslow studied what motivates people—what drives us to survive, to belong, to create, and to grow.
He believed that our needs build on one another, like steps on a ladder or layers in a pyramid.
Each layer has to be steady before we can climb higher.

He described it like this:

1. **Food and Physical Needs** – the basics of survival: air, water, rest, warmth, and shelter.

2. **Safety and Stability** – protection, health, and a sense of security in our surroundings.

3. **Love and Belonging** – friendship, affection, family, compassion, and the comfort of being seen.

4. **Esteem and Purpose** – dignity, confidence, respect, and a feeling of worth.

5. **Self-Actualization** – the longing to grow, to create, to understand our purpose, and to become whole.

Maslow explained that when the lower layers aren't met—when we're hungry, sick, unsafe, or too exhausted—the higher ones become difficult to reach. You can't think about art when your stomach is empty. You can't offer love when you're shivering in fear. You can't find peace when your body is in pain.

That isn't selfishness; it's simply how we're made. And that truth alone can soften the way we judge ourselves — and others.

This eases the shift into your loving/receiving awareness. And that's something worth remembering— sometimes love doesn't leave us; it just can't climb past the ache.

But here's the hopeful part: once those basic needs are met—once we feel safe, rested, and seen—love begins to rise again like a plant turning toward the sun.

Maslow called the highest point *self-actualization*, but really, it's what you and I would call becoming whole. It's when we begin to care not only about surviving, but about giving.
And maybe that's why the smallest acts of kindness often come from those who've known struggle—they remember what it means to need.

Now, when we think about this in the context of pain, we see how easily love can slip down a few steps. Chronic illness, grief, or fear of loss can drop us right back to the base—not because we've failed, but because life has gotten heavier.

When that happens, our first job isn't to force love to the top again.

It's to tend to the lower layers—to rest, to heal, to eat, to breathe, to let others care for us.
Only then can love climb again.

Once love finds its footing, it looks for somewhere to land. That's where compassion begins—where care moves from theory to touch.

And if someone offers to bring soup, just let them. Refusing kindness doesn't make us stronger—it only makes the soup cold.

So if we meet someone whose kindness has gone quiet, let's remember:
Maybe they're not unkind—maybe they're hungry, mourning, or just worn thin.
Their foundation may be shaking.
And perhaps the question for us is simple: *Can we love someone enough to let them rebuild before asking them to give?*

The Work of Compassion

Compassion is often misunderstood. It isn't a feeling we wait for—it's an act we choose.
It's what happens when we care enough to notice and stay long enough to help.
It's the courage to show up for another person, even when it costs us a little of our comfort.

When the body aches and the heart grieves, the world shrinks. People stop reaching out, not out of pride but for protection.
Sometimes pain builds walls so high that even kindness can't find a way through. That's why compassion must be patient — it can't demand entry. We think no one can

understand what we're feeling, or worse, that we might burden them if they try. Yet, refusing comfort doesn't save us — it only deepens the ache.

The truth is, love has two directions: giving and receiving.
Pain can make us forget not only the first but also the second one.
But accepting care isn't weakness; it's another form of courage—the courage to let someone else help carry the weight.
And maybe that's something we could all practice a little more—letting love come toward us instead of always trying to send it out.

Sometimes compassion looks heroic, but more often it's small and practical.
It's the hand that steadies someone's arm, the coffee poured for a neighbor, the quiet "How are you?" we asked twice because we care and really want to know.
It's showing up for someone else even when our own hearts are tired.

And if that coffee spills, well, maybe that's just life's way of saying "you're human." We laugh, wipe the counter, and keep caring anyway.

We've all seen older faces that seem to have forgotten how to smile.
Not because they don't feel love, but because life has taken its toll—pain in the joints, empty chairs at the table, memories that ache more than they comfort.
Their smiles are still there, just resting.

That's why the old saying stays true: "Be kind; everyone you meet is fighting a hard battle."
The trick is remembering that their battle may not be visible.
And maybe—just maybe—ours isn't either.

The Lion and the Thorn

There's a story I've always loved—an old one from Aesop, retold countless times.

A man named Androcles fled his master and hid in the forest.
Weary, hungry, and frightened, he found a cave for shelter. Inside, he saw a lion limping toward him, its paw swollen and bleeding.

Androcles froze, expecting to be devoured. But the lion stopped and lifted its paw as if asking for help.
Androcles saw a thorn buried deep in the flesh.
Trembling, he pulled it out and wrapped the paw with a strip of cloth torn from his tunic.
The lion licked his hand and lay quietly beside him.

For a time, they lived together—two frightened creatures finding comfort in each other's company.
Eventually, Androcles was captured and sentenced to death, thrown to the lions in the arena.

When the lion was released, it charged forward, but instead of attacking, it stopped and pressed its head against him.
It was the same lion.

The crowd gasped, and the emperor pardoned them both.

That's the kind of story that stays with you.
It reminds us that compassion can move in both directions.
Sometimes we're Androcles, tending to another's wound.
Sometimes we're the lion, needing someone gentle enough to reach past our roar.
And in both moments, we're reminded that trust is the bridge between pain and peace.

Pain humbles the strong; love redeems the frightened. And in the quiet space between them, both are made whole again.

You can almost imagine that lion afterward—purring a little louder than before, maybe still limping, but finally at peace. Androcles probably never bragged again; I like to think they both just smiled a lot after that.

If we're honest, isn't that what we all want—to be seen, helped, and forgiven in the same breath?

When Healing Takes Time

Pain doesn't just live in the heart—it lodges in the body.
The old shoulder that tenses when we reach for a hug, the stomach that tightens from worry, the hand that trembles when grief returns.
The body remembers everything: the falls, the surgeries, the losses, the names we still whisper in prayer.
And when the body is tired, it asks the heart to rest too.

So, healing begins slowly.
A Day with less pain.

A moment of laughter that doesn't hurt.
A smile that feels almost natural again.

That's love behind walls—it never truly leaves; it just waits for us to open the gate.
And maybe that's our task—not to tear down every wall at once, but to make sure the door still swings both ways.

Because even if pain makes us slower, it can also make us softer.
And when we let that softness reach others, it becomes love in its truest, most human form.
Perhaps that's the quiet miracle of healing—it doesn't return us to who we were; it lets us become gentler than before.

When Love Learns to Limp

If courage taught us how to move through fear, then pain teaches us how to move through tenderness.
Both require patience. Both remind us we're still alive.
And maybe that's what this whole journey has been about—learning not just how to love others, but how to let love find us when we're hurting too.

So, let's keep walking gently—with our aches, our memories, our small acts of kindness—and remember that love doesn't end when the body falters.
It simply learns new ways to reach.

And if all we can manage some days is a smile through pain, then that smile is enough. Because behind it, love is still at work. Maybe that's love's final joke on pain—it teaches us to laugh again, even if the laugh wobbles a little. Besides, a crooked smile still counts—it just means life had a few good laughs at our expense, and we're still here to laugh back.

9 ½ Rusty

I know this man — his name is Rusty.

Rusty can make a bad day better just by walking onto it. He's got this grin that starts in his eyes before it ever reaches his mouth, and a way of talking that makes you feel like you've known him for years.

He says things like, *"Every day's a holiday, and every meal's a feast,"* and the way he says it makes you believe him. He doesn't say it to be funny — he lives it.

Now, Rusty used to be a rodeo clown. But if you call him that, he shakes his head and says, *"Bullfighter."* That's what they call themselves when they've been close enough to danger to know the difference. He says it with that cowboy pride, and I figure he's earned it.

He claims he's in the Rodeo Hall of Fame. Maybe he is. Maybe that's just one of his stories. With Rusty, you never really know, but the way he says it, you want to believe.

By the time I met him, he'd traded the arena for the job site. The kind of man who always has a bit of advice tucked away.

One morning, he looks over at me and says, "A.J., look, we gotta run to *work. When you run to the work, you get to choose the job. Everybody thinks you're running to work because you're anxious to get there, and you're tearing the bone out of it — but when you get there first, you get to choose the job."*

He says, *"Let's just get started — knowing how comes later."*

He isn't fancy, but he's wise. Not the kind of wisdom you find in books — the kind that smells like dust and coffee and comes from paying attention.

Rusty can talk to anyone — doesn't matter what color, what creed, what age.

Rusty didn't harbor any hate inside him, but when we met people who did, he got along with them just the same. I asked him about it. *"Some folks are just like that,"* he says, *"They are small, but they were brought up that way; they don't know any better."*

We walk the job together, and he stops to talk to every soul we pass. He asks, *"Where you from?"* and before they can finish answering, he grins and says, *"I fought bulls there."* Then he jumps into that old auctioneer routine — *"How 'bout, how 'bout, how 'bout you? Twelve-fifty, who's got twelve-fifty, thirteen, thirteen?"*
Hands flying, voice bouncing like a drumroll. And everyone — even the quiet ones — starts to laugh.

That's Rusty's real work: reminding people that life's lighter than we think.
Rusty told me, *"People hire me to lift the morale."*

One day, a man died on the job — a good man, one everybody liked. They sent us home early. It was quiet in the truck for a while, just the road noise between us. Then Rusty said,

"You know, when you're young, you go to a lot of weddings. When you get older, you go to a lot of funerals."

He said it like he was talking about the weather, but it landed heavy.

I tell that story sometimes to people who are mourning — not the newly grieving, but the ones who've been carrying it a long while. I tell them about Rusty: his laugh, his sayings, his bullfighter pride, his kindness.

Then I ask if they know what the moral of the story is. They usually say,

"When you're young, you go to weddings; when you're old, you go to funerals."

I tell them, "No.

The moral to this story is now you know who Rusty is."

He died at forty-two of brain cancer.

After Rusty was gone, *I realized that grief is never one story. It lives in many voices — some we've met, and some we only imagine.* And sometimes those voices come from places we never expected.

Here is another story.

There was once a woman who lived through too much history.
She lost her home, her family, even her country — yet she carried one thing no one could take: *her voice.*

When people came to her in grief, she told them stories. Not fairy tales, but the kind that begin, *"Once, I too was broken..."Her stories didn't erase pain; they named it. And by naming it, she tamed it.*

Children grew quiet when she spoke. Old men wept. Strangers found each other in her words.

Years later, when she herself grew frail, she wrote one last story — for her daughter, who had gone ahead of her into silence.

In it, she wrote: *"If love cannot change death, then at least let it remember."* She understood something we all learn sooner or later: remembrance is a form of love.

And because she wrote it, *the world remembered too.*

Sometimes, when we hear words like hers, we remember that storytelling itself is an act of love — one heart reaching across time to steady another. In every shared story, we borrow someone else's courage and offer a bit of our own in return. *And that's how remembrance becomes living again.*

There's a line from John Green's book The Anthropocene Reviewed that stays with me. **He wrote**, *"We are here because we are here."*

At first, it sounds almost like nonsense — a loop with no way out. But maybe that's what makes it true. *It means we exist because others did. We stand where they stood. We breathe air that they once breathed. We carry forward what they could not finish.*

The ones who came before us never really left. *They're still here* — in the way we speak, in the habits they handed down, in the jokes that still make us laugh even when we can't remember who first told them.

When I think of Rusty, I can still hear his auctioneer's rhythm — that quick, rolling sound that made a whole room lighter.
When I think of others I've lost, I still feel them near. Not ghosts. Not memories, exactly. Something quieter, steadier — the way love lingers in the air after it's spoken.

That's what love does. It keeps the gone from being gone.

The Day of the Dead understands this.
It teaches that *no one is ever truly lost if they're remembered. Every candle, every song, every photograph says the same quiet truth:* **You still belong with us.**

Maybe that's what John Green meant — that being here is not just about existence, but about connection.
We are here because they were here.
Their lives made space for ours. Their hopes built our foundations. *Their stories shaped the ones we're still telling.*

When I hold on to my pain, it isn't because I'm afraid to move on.
It's because that pain is proof — the shape love takes when it refuses to disappear.

And when I speak their names, even softly, they answer in the only way they can:
In warmth, in quiet courage, in the small ways love keeps showing up.

We are here because they are here.
And they are here because we remember.

Do you remember in The Lion King when Mufasa said *that the great kings of the past look down on us from the stars, and when we feel alone, we only need to remember?*

87

It isn't just a comforting thought for a child.
It's a moral truth: remembrance itself is compassion.
To remember is to keep love alive, to refuse indifference, to say you still matter.

So maybe that's what all of this means — John Green's line, Mufasa's wisdom, the altars and candles, the ache that won't leave.
We are not separate from the ones we've lost.
We are their continuation.
Their laughter still moves through our breath, their lessons still shape our choices, and their kindness still echoes in every compassionate act we carry forward.

We are here because they are here. Their light is the one we carry, even on days we feel dim.
And when our time comes, others will be too — remembering, laughing, and carrying the light forward once more.

10. The Measure of Our Humanity

Maybe this is the right time to talk about the quiet agreements that hold us together — the unspoken social contract that makes life possible.

When we were young, we thought freedom meant doing whatever we wanted. But the longer we live, the more we see that freedom without care is chaos. We begin to understand that the small courtesies — patience, honesty, respect — are what make shared life possible. Somewhere along the way, we learn that freedom and kindness aren't opposites — they depend on each other."

The Social Contract

You may have heard the phrase *social contract*. It sounds like something from a philosophy class — but it's really just an understanding that each of us lives under every day.

It goes something like this: We are all born free, but we agree to give up a little of that freedom so that everyone can live safely together.

That's the social contract.

It's the reason we follow rules even when no one's watching — not out of fear, but because we believe others will do the same.

We agree not to steal so our own doors can stay unlocked. We stop at red lights so everyone gets home alive. We wait our turn, pay our share, lend a hand — not because someone's keeping score, but because it keeps the world from falling apart before lunch. And most days, that's a pretty reasonable goal.

It's a trade between freedom and safety, but also between self and community. When it works, it builds trust — the invisible thread that lets us walk down the street without fear. When it breaks, fear rushes in to fill the space.

And that's why decency matters most when it's inconvenient. The real measure of a society isn't how it treats its strong, but how it tends its tired, its sick, its unseen.

We all feel that contract in our bones, even if we never put it into words. It's why we nod to strangers, hold doors, or help a neighbor carry something heavy. (Ha, not every time, but we try.) It's the human promise: *I'll look out for you, because I hope you'll look out for me.*

Sometimes people break that promise. They lie, they take, they hurt. But when they don't — when someone surprises us with unexpected kindness — we remember that the social contract still stands.

The Human Crisis

Albert Camus once told a story in his 1946 speech, *The Human Crisis.*
He spoke of a man tortured by a Nazi officer. Later, that same officer tended the man's wounds and gave him

water. Camus wasn't excusing cruelty — he was revealing something strange and human: even in the darkest hearts, a spark of decency can flicker through.

That moment matters. It tells us that goodness isn't something we're taught; it's something we remember. We are born with it, though life often teaches us to forget.

It also reminds us that the line between good and evil doesn't run between nations or classes; it runs through every human heart. We are capable of both cruelty and care, often within the same breath. The miracle is that some people continue to choose to care.

Maybe that's what civilization really is — not progress, not technology, but the daily renewal of our social contract: the quiet decision to be kind despite the reasons not to be.

The Measure of Strength

It's easy to think morality lives in laws or doctrines, but those are only scaffolds — empty frames until someone fills them with compassion. What gives them meaning are the people who, day after day, do what's right when no one would blame them for looking away.

We don't often think of decency as a form of courage, but it is. Every time we choose understanding over judgment, or patience over pride, we strengthen the fragile thread that holds us together. That thread is invisible, but it's the strongest thing we have — the living cord of our shared promise.

If we look back, we'll remember Kant's reminder — that we must treat people as ends in themselves, never as means to our own ends. We talked about that before, but here it deepens. Because what Kant gave us wasn't just a rule — it was a mirror. It asks us to see the person beside us not as someone to use, fix, or outsmart, but as someone walking their own road with dignity equal to our own.

In the language of this chapter, that's what the social contract truly protects — not just safety, but respect. It's the understanding that civilization survives only as long as we continue to see one another as full human beings, not just as roles, tools, or labels.

That's the measure of strength I believe in. Not the strength to dominate, but the strength to restrain; not the strength to shout, but the courage to listen. True strength has a kind face. It holds steady. It smiles, even when the world gives it reason not to.

And sometimes that quiet kind of strength — the kind that nods, forgives, or waits — changes more than a dozen loud speeches ever could.

The Bridgekeeper

There's an old story about a man who tended a bridge that spanned a wide river between two villages. He wasn't a soldier or a scholar, just a quiet worker whose job was to open and close the gates so travelers could pass.

Each morning, he rose before dawn, checked the ropes, and swept the boards clean. People crossed without ever noticing him. Some waved, most didn't. But the bridgekeeper kept at it — steady, invisible, reliable.

One day, the river flooded. The water rose, the wind howled, and pieces of driftwood battered the bridge. The man could have saved himself; no one would have blamed him. But he stayed, tying ropes, driving stakes, shouting to strangers to keep moving.

When the storm passed, the bridge still stood — barely — and the people crossed again as if nothing had happened. Only a few stopped to thank him. Most didn't even know who he was.

Still, every morning, he returned to his post.

That's the thing about moral strength — it rarely makes headlines. But it's what keeps the world from collapsing. The bridgekeepers of life — the teachers, nurses, neighbors, the quiet helpers — they're the ones holding civilization together one small act at a time.

They don't carry banners, and they don't need applause. Their reward is the knowledge that the bridge still stands.

The Bridge Between Us

Maybe the social contract isn't just an idea written in books — maybe it's the quiet way we keep choosing one another.

We can't see it, but we live by it every day — in the ways we wait, forgive, and share. It's what turns freedom into fellowship, and strangers into neighbors.

Each time we hold the door, stop to listen, or simply smile at someone who looks worn thin, we renew that contract — not with words, but with presence. We remind the world, *I still believe in us.*

And that's no small thing. In a time when shouting often drowns out listening, every act of patience is a small rebellion of hope. And every bit of decency we offer teaches others to do the same. Every laugh we share, every bit of warmth we give freely, keeps the contract alive.

We'll never keep it perfectly. We'll fail, lose patience, or look away when we should have stayed. But that's the beauty of this agreement — it isn't carved in stone; it's written in the heart, rewritten each morning in how we treat whoever crosses our path.

Maybe that's the point: the social contract isn't about law — it's about trust. It's the quiet belief that kindness is not weakness, and decency is not naïve. It's our daily promise that life will be better, not just for me, but for *us.*

Because at its core, that contract is made of something far stronger than rules — it's made of respect, compassion, and courage. It's the faith that we can be free *and* good, that we can walk our own road without forgetting to leave the bridge standing behind us.

And maybe that's the real test of a good life — not how much we got, but how often we remembered the people walking beside us. We can't fix every bridge, and we can't carry every burden, but we can look at the road we've crossed and ask, *Did I make it easier for someone else to pass?*

That's the heartbeat of the social contract — the quiet promise that we are stronger together than alone, and that kindness is not a dream but a discipline.

So as we leave this part of the road, maybe we can ask ourselves — not with guilt, but with curiosity — *what kind of bridgekeeper am I?*
Do I repair, or do I walk past? Do I listen, or do I rush ahead?

Because the truth is, we don't just inherit this world; we build it daily with the way we treat one another.
And when kindness becomes habit — not theory, not duty, but habit — that's when civilization begins to feel like home again.

Maybe that's where we'll go next:
How to keep our kindness strong without losing ourselves —
How to build bridges without forgetting to rest on our own shore once in a while.

11. The Boundaries of Love

We've spent time talking about love in its many shapes —
love that forgives, love that grows, love that survives
pain. But love, like anything alive, needs space to breathe.
Too much giving without rest, and even the best
intentions start to fray. You can feel it in your shoulders
first, that quiet weight that no amount of coffee fixes.
Even laughter sounds a little thin.

There's a term for that in the medical world —
compassion fatigue. It's what happens when we keep
pouring from the cup long after it's empty. Nurses know
it. Teachers know it. Parents, friends, and caregivers know
it too. It's not selfishness; it's human limitation dressed in
good intentions.
Even saints, I suspect, needed naps. Maybe that's why
halos float — they're taking a break.

When care becomes exhaustion, something subtle
shifts. We still love, but it hurts to show it. We still want to
give, but there's nothing left to give. That's where
boundaries come in — not as walls, but as the quiet edges
that keep love from spilling out and leaving us dry.

What Boundaries Really Mean

We previously talked about loving ourselves — not out of pride, but out of respect. Boundaries are how we protect that respect in action. They are love with structure, kindness with form.

A river needs its banks; love needs its shape. Without those edges, the current floods everything, and even the fertile fields drown.

Boundaries aren't built because love has faded; they're built because we've learned how to love without losing ourselves. They're not a sign of selfishness but of maturity — a way of saying, *I will keep giving, but not at the cost of becoming empty.*

And maybe that's what self-love looks like when it grows up — not mirrors and affirmations, but the quiet courage to say, *this much, and no more.*
We learned that lesson early, although we didn't call it that at the time.
We called it *honor* — the strength to hold steady without harm.

The Giver and the River

There's a story I once heard about a woman who drew water from the river every morning for her village. She filled their pots, washed their clothes, helped the elders drink — day after day until her shoulders ached and her hands blistered.

The people praised her kindness, but one morning, she simply didn't rise. The village panicked — the river seemed to have run dry. They waited days before realizing what had happened: she was the one who kept the path clear. Without her, the reeds had grown thick, and the stream could no longer reach them.

When she finally recovered, she didn't return to her old routine. Instead, she built a schedule. She worked in the mornings, rested at midday, and let the river flow on its own when she couldn't.
And the water found its way again.

Love dries up not from selfishness, but from exhaustion.
The river doesn't run out of care — it runs out of rain. And we do too, when we forget to rest.

The Science of Compassion Fatigue
Doctors and psychologists call it *compassion fatigue* — when empathy becomes an overuse injury of the heart. It doesn't mean we've stopped caring; it means we've cared for too long without taking a break.

It happens to those who stand close to suffering: nurses, parents, teachers, counselors, friends — people whose hearts run toward pain instead of away from it. Over time, that constant nearness to struggle can leave us numb, irritable, or simply hollow. We can't pour endlessly; the cup cracks.

Anyone who's sat alone after caring for someone knows the sound — the long, hollow sigh that isn't quite defeat, just the body whispering, *enough for now.*

Maslow taught us that we must meet our basic needs before we can climb to higher ones — safety before belonging, rest before compassion.

It's a good reminder: we can't offer warmth when we're freezing.
We can't heal others when we haven't slept in days.

The monk Thich Nhat Hanh once taught that *when we breathe calmly, we do not abandon the world; we steady it.* Sometimes the kindest act of compassion isn't showing up for everyone else — it's taking a breath long enough to stay present when we do.

How often, I wonder, do we mistake depletion for devotion?

Rest, like love, always finds its way into a story. Maybe that's why every culture hides its wisdom in parables about balance.

The Girl and the Gate

There's an old story, simple as a breeze, that reminds us of balance.
A girl lived at the edge of a wide field filled with flowers. She loved them dearly and left the garden gate open so her neighbors could come and enjoy them. For a while, everyone did — until the field turned to trampled dirt.

She wept for what was lost. Then, in her grief, she locked the gate completely. No one could enter. The flowers grew back, but the joy didn't. The air grew still.

One day, an old woman passing by asked, "Why not open it halfway?"

So she did.

From that day on, the garden bloomed again — not because everyone could enter, but because she had learned when to close the gate and when to open it.

Love doesn't mean leaving the gate open to every storm. It means knowing when to close it long enough to heal.

Quiet love — the kind we discussed earlier — needs space to breathe. Without boundaries, even gentleness turns frantic.

The Kind "No"

There's a kind of courage in the gentle *no*.
It's not defiance; it's dignity. It's the soft voice that says, I can't do that right now, but I still care.

When was the last time we said a kind no, not to push someone away, but to keep our hearts steady enough to stay kind tomorrow?

That's the kind of moral strength we once called *honor* — not the noisy kind that fights to win, but the quiet kind that knows its own limits.
As we saw in *The Measure of Our Humanity*, strength isn't domination — it's restraint.

A Lakota tradition teaches that humility and balance are what hold the world steady. That same wisdom lives in every "no" spoken with love.
You can't water every field; some days it's enough just to sit by the well and wave to the neighbors.

And maybe that's the trick: to trust that love still exists even when we rest.

What if saying no kindly is another way of saying yes to peace?

The Balance of Joy

And before we finish talking about limits, we should reflect on what keeps the heart light enough to honor them.

We've learned courage and compassion, but both tire without joy.
Joy is love's way of stretching its legs — a reminder that life isn't all duty and ache.

A wise poet once said that joy is the soul's laughter.
And maybe that's the truth of it— joy is what keeps love human.

If compassion fatigue is the body's warning, laughter is its cure.
It's love reminding us not to take ourselves so seriously.

We can't always save the world, but we can smile at it.
And sometimes that's enough.

Love with Edges, Heart with Form

If the *social contract* keeps the world in balance, then personal boundaries keep our hearts in balance. Both depend on trust — one with others, one within ourselves.

We've walked this road together — through pain, courage, compassion, and rest — and all along the way, love has changed shape but never its purpose.
It learns, it bends, it builds edges, and grows soft again.

Maybe love isn't endless after all — maybe it's renewable.
And renewal takes rest, honesty, and a good laugh or two.

So if someone asks what you're doing when you finally stop to breathe, tell them this:
"I'm still loving — just from the recharge setting."

Halfway Open Gates

Love can give, but it can also rest.
It can reach out, but it can also return home.
It can say yes, but it must also learn to say no.

Maybe that's the lesson this time — that compassion without care for ourselves isn't noble; it's incomplete. Boundaries aren't barriers; they're the architecture of endurance.

And as we keep walking this road together — knees aching, hearts open, laughter somewhere between the two — maybe we'll remember that the world doesn't need us to burn out.

So if you're tired, rest. The world won't end while you breathe. It might even heal a little, waiting for you to come back.

It just needs us to stay kind, stay human, and stay long enough to keep the gate halfway open.

12. The Inner Voice: Your Life Companion

There's a voice inside us that isn't just conscience — it's company.
It doesn't only tell us right from wrong; it helps us make sense of who we are. It's the part of ourselves we can't escape — the one we debate with, explain ourselves to, and lean on when life turns quiet.

This voice isn't dramatic or divine. It's steady. It asks questions we'd rather ignore and forgives us more often than we deserve. Sometimes it's gentle; sometimes it stings. But it's always there, waiting for us to listen.

We can call it conscience if we like, but it's more than that. It's the "self" that lives behind the noise — the part of us that still asks, *Is this right? Is this me?*

It's the conversation that never really ends.

The Voice We Live With

Socrates once said it is better to suffer wrong than to do wrong.
Hannah Arendt, writing centuries later, agreed — not from piety, but from experience. She said the reason was simple: when we do wrong, we must live with the person who did it — *ourselves.*

That's the real punishment — not guilt, not shame, but the quiet discomfort of being trapped in bad company when that company is you.

Arendt explained that thinking — honestly thinking — means engaging in an internal dialogue, and that morality begins in this internal conversation. When we silence it, when we drown it out with noise, slogans, or the comfort of crowds, we risk forgetting who we are.

She once warned that evil often begins not in rage or malice, but in thoughtlessness — in people who stop speaking with themselves long enough to follow orders, to blend in, to go along.
But she also believed that goodness begins the same way — in conversation. In the willingness to think, to question, to ask, *Can I live with this?*

That voice doesn't shout. It doesn't argue. It simply waits for the world to quiet down long enough to be heard.
And when it speaks, it sounds an awful lot like you.

Frodo's Ring —Tolkien's Echo
Would you want Frodo's ring — you know, the one that makes you invisible any time you wanted?

Imagine it — no one could see what you did. No one could judge, scold, or hold you accountable. You could slip past rules, skip apologies, and no one would ever know.

Tempting, isn't it?

Long before Tolkien, Plato told a similar story. In one of his dialogues, he described a shepherd named Gyges who found a ring that could make him invisible. When he realized its power, he used it to steal, seduce, and eventually murder the king. Plato's question was simple — and unsettling:

If we could do wrong without consequence, would we still choose to be good?

It's the same question Tolkien asked, only dressed in myth and hobbits. In *The Lord of the Rings*, the magic isn't freedom — it's temptation. Every person who wears the ring begins to believe they can control it, but the truth is, it controls them.

We like to think we'd be different, that we'd use the ring for good — maybe to right a few wrongs or play a harmless trick or two. But power rarely stays harmless for long. As soon as we start deciding which rules we can bend, the voice inside us — the same one Socrates and Arendt spoke of — starts to fade into the background.

And here's the quiet danger: when we can no longer hear ourselves, we can justify almost anything.

Would we still recognize ourselves if no one else could see us?
Would we act with the same kindness, the same honesty, if no one would ever know?

The ring makes a fine story because it reminds us that morality isn't about being watched — it's about being *whole.*
If we only do good when someone's looking, we're not being moral — we're just being careful.

That brings to mind a conversation I once had with my nephew, John. He's a bright, curious young man with that mix of humor and honesty that makes you proud and worried all at once. One evening, he told me about a television series he'd been watching called *The Boys*.

In that show, people with superpowers act like heroes in public but are cruel, selfish, even monstrous behind the scenes. John shook his head and said, "That's just how people would be if they had power."

I thought about that for a long moment. Then I said, "Maybe that's how *some* people would be. But not you."

He laughed, a little embarrassed, and said, "How do you know?"

"Because," I told him, "you already have power — the power to hurt or to help, to mock or to understand, to turn away or to show up. And you don't use it for harm."

He went quiet then, thinking. And so did I.

Power doesn't have to corrupt. It only does when we stop listening to the voice inside — the one that keeps us human.
If you gave John that ring — the one that makes you invisible — I don't believe he'd use it for evil.
I don't think most of us would.
Because beneath all our mistakes and noise, that voice still whispers: *You know better.*

Frodo's real power wasn't carrying the ring; it was resisting it.
And maybe ours is the same — not to rule, but to

remember.
To remember who we are, even when no one else can see.

The Companion We Build

We began this road with Socrates and Arendt, but their voices keep returning, don't they? They remind us that philosophy isn't something ancient — it's the way we live with ourselves today. And maybe that's where the real work begins — not with power, but with the voice that keeps us company when the noise fades.

When Socrates said it's better to be wronged than to do wrong, he was naming a quiet kind of peace — the peace of a clear conscience.
Hannah Arendt, writing in another troubled age, discovered the same truth: the hardest person to live with is the one who has done harm. She explained that when you do wrong, you must live afterward with the one who did it — *yourself.*

That's the quiet consequence we forget. No judge, no jury, no headline — just the voice inside that will not lie for us.
That voice may go silent when the crowd grows loud, but it never truly leaves.
It waits for quiet.

You can ignore it, drown it, or debate it, but sooner or later, it speaks again — not as punishment, but as recognition:
This is who I am, and this is who I've become.

That's not conscience alone. It's something deeper — a lifelong companion. The one who's been there for every choice, every small surrender, every kindness we thought no one saw.

It's the part of us that knows before we rationalize, that hesitates before we excuse, that winces before we wound.

Most of us aren't haunted by grand sins — we're haunted by the little betrayals: the time we stayed silent when we should've spoken, or looked away when someone needed us. The moments when the voice said, *Don't*, and we did anyway.

Arendt once wrote that evil often begins not with monsters, but with people who stop thinking — people who quiet that inner dialogue long enough to follow the crowd.

But the opposite is also true: decency begins when we think again. When we pause before reacting, when we ask ourselves —

"Can I live with this choice?"

It's not a rulebook. It's a mirror.

And like all mirrors, it shows us what we'd rather not see — the distance between our values and our behavior. But it also shows us something else: the chance to close that distance, one honest act at a time.

We talk about living with others, but the truth is, we also have to live with ourselves.

That's why Socrates said he'd rather suffer injustice than commit it — because it's easier to live with pain than with self-contempt.

And maybe that's wisdom's simplest form: knowing that your own company should be worth keeping.

So the question isn't only "What kind of world do we want to live in?"
It's "What kind of person do we want to live *with*?"

Because one day, when the noise settles and the crowd moves on, that's who will still be sitting beside you.

The Person We Keep

Maybe that's the heart of it — learning to live with the one who knows us best.

We can fool a boss, a neighbor, even the mirror for a time, but not that quiet witness who walks beside us from beginning to end.
It's the one who speaks in small questions: *Why did you say that? Why did you turn away?*

We've all had that conversation more times than we'd like to admit — while brushing our teeth, driving alone, or staring at the ceiling at 2 a.m. The voice never yells; it just asks again, patient and familiar, waiting for us to answer a little better next time.

And sometimes in small mercies: *It's all right. You tried.*

That voice isn't there to scold us — it's there to steady us. It asks only that we keep it honest company. Maybe that's friendship in its truest form — a self that still roots for us, even after hearing every excuse we've ever made. When we do, life becomes less about perfection and more about peace — not the peace of never erring, but the peace of knowing we've done what we could, as kindly as we could.

We spend our lives surrounded by others, but the longest conversation we'll ever have is with ourselves. And like any good friendship, it takes patience, humor, and forgiveness to keep it alive.

And if we ever think we've finally mastered the conversation, that's probably the moment our inner voice chuckles and says, "Really? Let's go over that one more time."

So maybe wisdom isn't found in answers at all — but in keeping the conversation open.
In asking again and again, *Can I live with this?*
And if the answer is yes, then perhaps that's what it means to live rightly.

13. The Circle Beyond Sight

If you stop for a moment, you can almost feel it — the quiet bustle of other lives going on beside ours.
Someone wakes to feed a baby.
Someone worries about rent.
Someone laughs so hard it shakes the walls.

We only see a small corner of this great world. Most days, we move among the few faces we know, and it's easy to forget that beyond our little circle are people just as real, just as hopeful, just as hungry for love.

Caring for those we can't see doesn't come easy. But it's one of the ways we grow up inside — when our concern stretches beyond our sight.
It starts with imagination: *what if that person far away were my brother, my mother, my child?*

The Dalai Lama once said he finds it easy to love others because he believes they may have been his family in another life. You don't have to believe in reincarnation to feel the wisdom in that — we're all made of the same breath.

Maybe that's the truest kind of family there is.

A Mirror of Reason

In 1972, philosopher Peter Singer wrote *"Famine, Affluence, and Morality."* It was a response to a devastating famine in East Bengal. Singer's question was haunting but straightforward: *Why do we, who live in comfort, allow so many to die from hunger, when we could prevent it with such small sacrifices?*

He offered a scenario:

"If you were walking past a shallow pond and saw a child drowning, would you wade in and save the child, even if it meant ruining your clothes?"

We all know the answer. Of course we would. No one would stand by and watch a child drown.

But then Singer asked:

"If you can save a child's life on the other side of the world by giving up a luxury — a new pair of shoes, a restaurant meal — should that matter less?"

It's the same principle, just at a distance.
The moral truth doesn't change because the suffering happens elsewhere.

"Singer's argument feels almost disarming in its clarity — he wasn't trying to shame us — he was trying to wake us.
If it's in our power to prevent something bad from happening, without giving up anything of comparable moral worth, then we ought to do it.

But Singer's real genius is not in his logic — it's in how quietly he makes us look in the mirror. He asks us to compare what we *believe* with what we *do*, and then he

112

leaves us with the discomfort of that gap.
He doesn't say we are evil — only that we are capable of being better.

Let's reflect for a moment.
How many times have we turned away from a story of suffering simply because it felt too far away to matter?
How many times have we thought, "What difference could I make?"
Maybe the difference is simply this — to not look away.

The Stranger on the Road

Long before Singer, another teacher faced the same question: *Who deserves our compassion?*
In the Gospel, a scholar of the law asked Jesus, "Who is my neighbor?" And Jesus answered with a story.

A man traveling from Jerusalem to Jericho is beaten and left for dead.
A priest passes him by. A Levite passes him by.
Then comes a Samaritan — a man from a people despised and distrusted. He stops, binds the wounds, carries the stranger to safety, and pays for his care.

"Which of these three," Jesus asked, "was a neighbor to the man who fell among thieves?"
The answer was obvious: the one who showed mercy.

And then he said, simply, "Go and do likewise."

Let's think about that. The story wasn't a lesson in charity; it was a redefinition of *neighbor*.
It shattered the tribal boundary and drew a new moral circle — one that included even the stranger, even the foreigner, even the enemy.

113

Jesus' story and Singer's argument say the same thing in two different languages:
The moral value of a life does not depend on closeness, culture, or creed. Distance changes our sight, not our responsibility.
The child in the pond, the wounded man on the road — both are our neighbors.

And yet, this widening of care always begins in the heart — in that small, human moment when we decide that someone else's pain belongs to us.

The Bow of the Heart
In many Eastern traditions, compassion is expressed not only in thought but in gesture.
When yogis meet, they place their hands together at the heart and bow their heads, saying *Namaste* — "I bow to the divine within you."

It's a simple act, yet it carries an entire philosophy: that the same sacred spirit lives in every being.
To bow is to recognize that spirit, not as a symbol, but as truth. This gesture isn't exotic — it's simply a reminder of what we forget too easily: we belong to each other.

Imagine if we lived that way — if every encounter were a silent acknowledgment that the life before us carries the same light we do.
We might speak less harshly, judge less quickly, and forgive more easily.

This bow is not about submission; it's about equality — a wordless reminder that we are part of one shared holiness. Whether we call it God, humanity, or consciousness, the meaning is the same: *we are one life, appearing in many forms.*

"He Ain't Heavy, He's My Brother"

There's a song — you probably know it — *"He Ain't Heavy, He's My Brother."*
It's a song about carrying another's burden, and how, when we truly care, it doesn't feel heavy at all.

Let's smile and think about that for a moment. Imagine a world where we each carried someone else's load just a little — not out of obligation, but out of love. How light would the world become?
How much less lonely?

I remember once, Darla and I saw a woman at the grocery store struggling with more bags than arms. We each grabbed a few and walked her to her car. It took two minutes, maybe less, but the laughter that followed rode with us all the way home. Funny how something that small can make a day feel lighter.

When the song says, *"the road is long, with many a winding turn,"* it's reminding us that life is already hard enough.
But when we walk together — when we remember that the stranger beside us is not heavy, just human — the road feels shorter.

The Road We Share

You know, life's a long road. Twists, turns, uphill climbs, and those long, quiet stretches where all you can hear are your own footsteps. Along the way, you meet people who walk beside you for a while, and others you only pass once. But every so often, someone stumbles, and that's when we remember what the old song said: *He ain't heavy, he's my brother.*

There's something right about that line. When you help carry another person's load, somehow your own feels lighter. Maybe that's the secret that all the great teachers were trying to tell us — that compassion doesn't drain us; it fills us.

It's the same lesson we've met before — the courage from earlier chapters, the quiet love behind walls — all of it leading here, to a compassion that doesn't stop at the edge of our sight.

I think about what Singer said, and about the Samaritan on that dusty road, and the yogi who folds his hands and bows. They're all saying the same thing in different tongues: we belong to one another.

So let's imagine, just for a moment, that everyone we meet — the tired cashier, the neighbor who keeps to himself, the stranger halfway around the world — has, in some way we can't quite remember, been part of our family. Maybe they were. Perhaps they still are.

And when we see them that way, something softens in us. We speak kinder. We listen longer. We forgive quicker. We start to notice that the world feels smaller, warmer, more familiar — as if we've all been walking the same road a very long time.

We've all carried someone and been carried in return. That's the rhythm of the road — give, receive, rest, repeat.

So if you ever wonder how far your compassion should reach, maybe the answer is simple: as far as your imagination can see. Because in the end, every burden we lift, every kindness we give, every time we look at someone and think *he ain't heavy* — we make the world a little more like home.

14. Why Distance Makes a Difference

In the last chapter, we stood beside Peter Singer's pond and watched a child struggle in shallow water.
We nodded along when he asked whether we'd step in to save that child—even if it meant muddy shoes or ruined plans. Of course, we would.
Singer's question was never really about ponds; it was about *reach*. If compassion means anything, it must stretch past what we can touch.

But once the page closes and the thought experiment fades, something curious happens.
The world rushes back in. Bills, chores, headlines, fatigue. Our compassion, so clear in theory, starts to thin out like morning fog.

The hard truth is this: moral clarity comes fast, emotional stamina does not. It isn't hypocrisy; it's human nature. We want to live up to Singer's logic, but our feelings don't travel as fast as our reason. The mind can picture a drowning child on the far side of the planet; the heart still looks for someone close enough to hold.

Let's be honest about that gap—not to excuse it, but to understand it.
If Chapter 12 was about the ideal, this one is about the real: why good people stumble between knowing and

118

doing, and how we can bridge that distance without losing heart.

The Boy in the Cape

A few years ago, a little boy named Miles Scott taught us what it looks like when compassion *crosses* the gap. You might remember him—the world called him *Batkid*. He was five, fighting leukemia, and his wish was to be Batman for a day.

When the request reached San Francisco, something extraordinary happened.
Police officers volunteered, city workers cleared streets, strangers made signs, and for one bright morning, the city turned into Gotham City.
Thousands cheered as a small figure in a black cape rode past in a Batmobile built from a rented Lamborghini.
Even the mayor played along, declaring, "Thanks to Batkid, Gotham is safe again."

For one child, the world became small; for one city, the world became kind.

And that, strangely enough, is the mirror image of Singer's pond.
His question asked why we don't rush to save the distant child.
Batkid showed what happens when distance disappears—when a name, a face, and a story pull the far into the near.

Psychologists have a name for this: *the identifiable victim effect.*
One face wakes us up where a thousand blur together.

Numbers numb us; stories move us.
Our compassion is built to respond to the particular, not the abstract.

It's the same reason Singer's argument cuts so deep. He shows us that morality can leap oceans, but he also exposes how our feelings lag behind our ethics. Batkid, on the other hand, reminds us that when compassion finds a doorway—a story, a smile, a child in a cape—it floods through with power enough to move a city.

The lesson isn't that we should feel guilty for caring more about one child than a million; it's that our empathy is wired for connection.
If Singer gives us the principle, Batkid gives us the pulse.

Why We Go Numb

We've all felt it—that quiet slide from caring to numbness. One story moves us, but ten make us tired.

It's not that our hearts shrink; it's that they fill up faster than we can empty them.
Psychologists call it *psychic numbing*. The more suffering we see, the less any single piece of it registers. The mind protects itself by going dim.

You might recall when we talked about the "quiet kind of love" that needs rest to stay alive. It's the same here. Compassion, too, can grow weary. When every channel, every scroll, every conversation brings another tragedy, the heart starts whispering, "Please, not another."

And then, almost without noticing, we drift into distance.
We skim headlines instead of reading them, murmur "how sad" instead of feeling it, and tell ourselves, "I just can't think about that right now."

We can smile at our own honesty here, can't we? Because we've all done it. It's part of being human in a noisy world.
Our compassion isn't broken; it's overloaded. It's like trying to hold rain in our hands—no matter how tight the grip, some of it will slip through.

But as we discussed before, awareness is the first step toward freedom. When we notice our empathy dimming, we can pause and say, *Ah, this is what tired love feels like.* And then we can rest, refill, and begin again.

When the Heart Gets Tired

There's a quiet kind of exhaustion that comes not from doing too little, but from *feeling too much.*
We've spoken about it before—how love and kindness, if left unchecked, can start to feel like heavy lifting. That's *compassion fatigue.*

It's what happens when the heart forgets to rest. When we pour and pour without pausing to refill.

Nurses know it. Teachers know it. Parents know it. Even those of us who simply try to stay informed feel it— the slow ache of too much sorrow, too often.

You might recall our talk about boundaries back in *The Boundaries of Love.*
We said love needs edges, not as walls but as banks that

keep the river from flooding. Compassion requires the same. Without edges, we overflow and lose direction.

I remember a nurse once told me, "Some days, I go home so tired I can't feel anything. And the next morning, I start again." She smiled as she said it, not proud or bitter—just honest.
That's compassion fatigue in its truest form: caring so much it empties you.

So what do we do?
First, we forgive ourselves for getting tired. The heart is not a machine; it's a living thing.
Second, we laugh a little. Because sometimes, the only cure for feeling everything is remembering joy still exists. Laughter isn't a betrayal of empathy—it's what keeps empathy alive.

And third, we rest with purpose.
We step away long enough to remember why we care at all. We fill our own cup, knowing it's not selfish—it's how we keep the well from going dry.

As we said before, compassion without rest becomes duty; compassion with rest becomes joy.

The Carer and the Cared For

If you recall, we met Nel Noddings earlier, and she gave us a way to see compassion as something alive between people.
Her image of **the Carer and the Cared For** isn't theory— it's a reminder of how moral life breathes.

The Carer offers attention—real attention, not the distracted kind that half-listens.

The Cared For responds, maybe with gratitude, maybe with a glance that says, "I see you."
That loop—attention and response—is what turns empathy into a relationship.

But distance breaks the loop.
When we can't see the person we're trying to help, when there's no reply, our caring starts to drift.
We send love out like a letter with no return address, and after a while, we stop mailing them.

Compassion needs feedback — a sign, however small, that someone is on the other side.

That's why the smallest tangible gestures matter— letters, photos, stories, names. They remind us that someone is *there,* receiving what we send.

Noddings would say this is how we keep compassion from becoming an idea instead of an act: we keep it personal. We find ways, even across miles, to make the invisible visible again.

As we talked about before, imagination is our ally here. It lets the faraway become familiar. The moment we picture the other person's life—even imperfectly—the circle of care begins again.

So the next time you give, or listen, or pray for someone far away, don't think of them as faceless. Picture them clearly.
And maybe smile, just a little, because you're rebuilding the bridge in your own way.

Bridging the Distance

Now we come to the real work—building bridges that can hold.

Bridges made of empathy, imagination, and deliberate choice.

We build them whenever we look past ourselves.
When we read one more story, even when it hurts.
When we choose to give, even when we'll never see the outcome.
When we pause long enough to feel something for someone we'll never meet.

Each act is a plank across the gap.
And as we've said before, the imagination is the carpenter of compassion. It's what turns the faraway into the near.

I remember Darla once sent a small donation to a relief fund after a flood overseas. She never mentioned it again. Months later, a short letter arrived — just a few lines from a woman who'd rebuilt her home and wanted to say thank you. Darla smiled and said, "It's strange, isn't it? We'll never meet, but somehow we've shared the same day." In that moment, I saw what distance can't erase — the simple connection between one heart reaching out and another reaching back. That's what connection is — strangers sharing the same day without ever meeting.

That's compassion traveling farther than sight.
It's not about measuring outcomes; it's about trusting that caring never really disappears—it changes hands.

And maybe that's how we balance Singer's question. We can't save everyone in the distant pond, but we can keep our hearts from drying up while we try.

The Bridge We Keep Building

If the last chapter invited us to widen our circle, this one reminds us to keep it strong.
Love that tries to cover the whole world at once will wear itself thin. Love that grows in steady circles—fed by rest, laughter, and renewal—can last a lifetime.

So let's be gentle with ourselves and honest about our limits.
Let's laugh when we trip, rest when we need to, and begin again when our hearts refill.

Because compassion isn't a test to pass; it's a rhythm to live by.
Some days, we'll feel everything. Other days, almost nothing.
Both are part of being human.

The goal isn't to feel it all—it's to keep caring, even when we can't feel it all.

So when you catch yourself growing numb, smile softly and say, *I'll rest, then I'll return.*
And when you're ready, take that next small step across the bridge—a message, a gesture, a moment of attention.

In time, those steps add up.
They build a road of mercy wide enough for others to walk beside you.

Because compassion isn't a feeling we chase — it's a direction we choose.

15. The Weight of Knowing

The road feels different now. We've been on this ride for a while, you and I — long enough that the sound of the tires purring against the pavement feels almost like breathing. The sun's lower now, the light softer, and there's that smell that comes after rain — clean and tired all at once.

We've talked about a lot on this road: love's quiet forms, courage that grows in stillness, the walls we build, the bridges we mend. Each chapter was a hill, a turn, a rest stop. And somewhere along the way, compassion stopped being an idea and became a kind of rhythm in how we move.

Do you remember when we first spoke about Maslow's pyramid — how love can't rise without a foundation beneath it? Or when Kant reminded us that people aren't means to our ends, but ends in themselves? Or when we stood with Peter Singer's child at the edge of that pond and felt the reach of care extending beyond sight?

Each lesson was another mile.
Now, the road ahead looks quieter, but heavier too — because once we *see* the world clearly, the weight of that sight never fully leaves us.

There's an old saying that goes, "We are responsible for what we know." And that's the tricky part of moral growth: once compassion opens our eyes, we can't easily close them again.

Sometimes I wish we could. It'd be nice, wouldn't it, to stop and rest our hearts? To just admire the sky without wondering who's hungry under it.
But that's not the kind of knowing this road gives us.
The kind we've built together — this language of care and conscience — doesn't let us unsee.

The Moment After Seeing
There's a strange stillness that comes after we *really* see something painful.
It's like that second of silence after lightning — when your breath catches, and the world feels both alive and fragile.

We've talked before about the *quiet kind of love* — the one that doesn't shout or rush, that listens instead. The kind that grows in the cracks of everyday life. That love is brave, but it's also tender, and it feels everything.
And the more we learn to feel, the more the world gives us to carry.

Maybe you've noticed it too. The more aware we become — of injustice, of loneliness, of how much pain sits quietly beside joy — the heavier it all feels. Awareness can be both a gift and a burden.

I think of Hannah Arendt here, the philosopher who said that evil often begins not with hatred, but with *thoughtlessness.* Her point wasn't about villains; it was

128

about us — the ordinary people who stop thinking, stop noticing, stop questioning.
Once we see the truth, we can't go back to being thoughtless.

That's the weight of knowing.
It's the moment after compassion opens our eyes, when we realize we'll never again be at ease inside ignorance.

We might smile at that thought, a little bittersweet. Because even though knowledge can feel heavy, it's also what makes love wiser.
As we talked about before, to love without awareness is sweetness; to love *with* awareness is strength.

Too Much Knowing

There's an old line that says, "The heart was made to hold a few sorrows at a time." These days, it feels like we're trying to hold the whole world.

Every hour brings another tragedy, another headline. One after another until all of them blur together.
And there we are — still pedaling, still scrolling, still whispering, "What can I possibly do about all this?"

You might remember when we talked about *compassion fatigue*. Back then, we said it wasn't failure — it was the heart's way of saying, *I need to breathe.*
That lesson hasn't gone anywhere. In fact, it feels more important now.

Knowing too much can numb us just as surely as feeling too little.
Our empathy has its limits, and when we cross them, the lights start to flicker. We tune out the world not because

129

we don't care, but because we care too much, too often, with too few moments to rest.

There's a soft humor in that, isn't there?
The same mind that can invent the wheel, split the atom, and fly to the moon still can't figure out how to process three sad stories in a row. We were built for villages, not galaxies.

And yet, we keep trying. We keep loving beyond what we're wired for. And maybe that's what makes this journey so human.

When the Heart Gets Tired
Do you remember what we said back in *The Boundaries of Love*? That even love needs edges, the way a river needs banks to keep it from flooding?
That truth has followed us here, too.

Compassion without boundaries becomes exhaustion. Compassion with boundaries becomes endurance.

I once spoke with a hospice nurse who told me, "Some days I go home and laugh until I cry. Not because it's funny, but because it's the only way to keep from breaking."
That's the heart's wisdom in disguise. It knows that joy, not guilt, is what keeps empathy alive.

We learned this before, but it bears repeating: love that never rests turns into duty, and duty without joy loses its warmth.
So when your heart grows tired, listen to it. Let it rest. Laugh. Do something beautiful for no reason.
Compassion isn't a contest; it's a rhythm.

Because here's the secret: every time you stop to breathe, the world doesn't lose your goodness — it just waits.

And when you're ready, you'll come back stronger, steadier, and maybe even smiling.

The Weight Shared

As we discovered back in *The Courage to Grow* and *The Measure of Humanity*, strength isn't about lifting alone. It's about finding someone who helps you carry the load.

The weight of knowing gets lighter when it's shared. When we tell a friend what we've seen. When we join hands in a cause. When we sit beside someone who understands that silence is sometimes the only language we have left.

Nel Noddings would say this is how we rebuild the circle of care — the Carer and the Cared For. Even truth itself needs a listener. Awareness alone can become despair; awareness shared becomes compassion.

So don't hold the world alone.

Tell someone about it. Laugh about it. Cry about it. Carry it together.

That's what all this learning has been about — not becoming saints, but staying human in a world that sometimes forgets how.

The Return to the Road

The road stretches on, quiet and familiar.

We've been riding for a while now, through the valleys of

fear and the hills of understanding. The sun is setting lower. The air's cooler. And maybe, for the first time, we don't mind the weight of the bike — we've learned to ride with it.

If you've been with me since the beginning, you might notice how the road itself has changed.
At first, it was about learning to love ourselves. Then, to love others. Then, to love across distance.
Now, it's about learning to *keep loving* after we've seen the world for what it is.

Maybe that's the final test of compassion — to stay open after knowing.

The philosopher Viktor Frankl once said that everything can be taken from a person except one thing: the freedom to choose one's attitude.
We can't control what we know. But we can choose what we do with it.

So as we ride, let's choose to carry the weight gently. Let's remember that the goal isn't to save the world, but to stay awake within it.

The bike squeaks more than it used to, and the road is a little rough, but that's alright. Every mile has mattered. And if you listen closely, you can almost hear the rhythm of the ride—the heartbeat of compassion itself, steady and human, carrying us forward.

Pedal easy here. We've earned the wind.

16. The Courage to Act

The road leans upward again. It isn't cruel—just honest. The wind presses against our chests, not enough to stop us, but enough to ask, *"Do you really mean to keep going?"*

We've been on this road a long while, you and I. We've coasted through valleys of quiet reflection, paused to breathe when compassion grew heavy, and found our rhythm again. But here, with the wind rising, the journey asks for something new. Not more thought, not more feeling—but *movement.*

It's funny how a little resistance brings everything back into focus. The pedals creak, the breath shortens, and suddenly the world feels real again. Wind doesn't let you pretend. It calls you to lean forward.

That's what this chapter is about—the moment when compassion stops being a thought and starts being a motion. When love, long practiced in theory, finally puts its feet on the pedals.

Virtue isn't something we're born with; it's something we *become* through practice. We don't wake up brave or generous. We grow into those things the way a musician learns an instrument—through repetition, through patience, through showing up again and again.

Love, too, is learned that way. Every act of care, every moment of restraint, every quiet kindness is another turn of the wheel. We wobble, we steady, we learn.

Practice, Not Perfection

When people talk about courage, they usually picture grand gestures—running into burning buildings, standing before armies, defying kings. But most courage doesn't look like that. Most of it looks like showing up, speaking gently, and not giving up when it'd be easier to walk away.

Moral strength doesn't arrive fully grown. It's practiced into being—like pedaling into a headwind until the muscles remember.

We practice love the same way.
The more we choose it, the easier it gets to choose again.

Think of the little habits that keep the heart in shape—the call you make even when you're tired, the apology you give even when pride aches, the patience you offer when no one's watching. Those aren't minor gestures. They're training sessions for the soul.

We become what we repeatedly do.
So if we practice kindness, we become kind.
If we practice empathy, we become compassionate.
If we practice love, we become love itself.

That's a comforting thought, isn't it?
We don't have to be perfect—we just have to keep practicing.

The road may be long, but every push of the pedal counts. Every small act of courage moves the wheel forward.

The Fear That Stops Us

Still, knowing what's right and doing it aren't the same thing.
Sometimes fear whispers, "Stay quiet." Sometimes comfort says, "Someone else will handle it."

You remember that story we told about the pond — the child in danger, and how easily we said we'd step in to help? But in real life, the water's colder, the crowd's watching, and suddenly our legs won't move.

It's called the bystander effect, but it's really just the human effect. We hesitate because we don't want to look foolish or alone. But every act of courage begins exactly there — in the pause between fear and motion, where we decide who we are.
And that's the hard truth: fear doesn't vanish with wisdom.
It fades only with *practice.*

Courage lives somewhere between recklessness and cowardice — the middle path where fear still exists, but obedience to fear does not.

Courage isn't loud; it's steady.
It's not the absence of trembling; it's trembling while still stepping forward.

You might smile, remembering times you froze before doing the right thing. I do too. But each time we manage

135

even a small step through that hesitation, we stretch our capacity to love.

And that's all moral courage really is—the muscle of love trained to move even when it's afraid.

Everyday Acts of Bravery

Most courage doesn't happen under spotlights.
It happens quietly—in break rooms, classrooms, kitchens, and street corners.

It's the employee who stands beside a co-worker being mistreated, knowing it might cost them something.
It's the parent who apologizes to a child instead of pretending they were right.
It's the teenager who invites the lonely kid to sit beside them at lunch.

No newspaper writes about these moments.
But they're the invisible scaffolding that holds the moral world together.

You remember *The Quiet Kind of Love,* when we talked about tenderness as strength?
That lesson belongs here, too.
Because the bravest thing most of us will ever do is stay kind when the world makes it easier not to.

Small choices are the daily practice of virtue.
I'd call them love's morning workout.

If goodness had a gym, it wouldn't be filled with weights—it'd be filled with moments: returning the wallet, forgiving the slight, listening longer, standing up kindly.

And each time we practice, we make the next act of love just a little easier.

Listening for the Inner Voice

By now, we've spoken often about the inner voice — the quiet companion of conscience that whispers when we drift.
In earlier chapters, we learned to hear it through rest, reflection, and compassion.
Now comes the test: can we still hear it when the wind is loud?

Moral action rarely comes from certainty; it comes from listening amid noise.
That inner voice doesn't shout — it hums, like the chain of a bike when it catches the right gear.
We know the sound when it comes: that click of alignment, that small surge of rightness.

The more we act on it, the clearer it becomes.
Each time we listen and follow through, the voice grows a little louder, a little steadier, until it becomes second nature.

That's how character is formed — through repetition until goodness becomes instinct.
We might just call it a habit of the heart.

The trick is not to wait for grand callings.
Listen for the little nudges — the "maybe I should call," "maybe I should help," "maybe I shouldn't walk away."
Those whispers are the start of courage.

The Companions of Courage

There's something comforting about realizing we don't ride alone.
You might recall back in *The Courage to Grow*, we learned that love grows in a relationship—now we see courage does too.

Even ancient teachers said friendship was the mirror of virtue.
We reflect each other's best selves, and in doing so, we keep our courage alive.

I once heard a cyclist describe riding into strong wind in a pack. The leader takes the brunt of it for a while, then moves aside, letting the next rider pull the group forward. That's how courage works among friends.
We take turns facing the wind.

Sometimes you'll be the one in front—speaking up, acting first.
Other times you'll draft behind someone else's bravery, gathering strength for your own next act.
That's not weakness; it's wisdom.
Courage is communal.

When love is practiced together, fear loses its hold.

When Courage Becomes Second Nature

The road levels out at last.
The air is still, but something inside us keeps moving. The hard miles, the climbs, the headwinds—they've all been part of the same lesson: the more we practice love, the more it becomes our way of being.

Before we reach that, I keep thinking of Darla at the grocery store once, quietly paying for a stranger's few missing dollars when their card failed. No cameras, no applause—just a soft, almost embarrassed kindness. That's the kind of courage that rehearses for bigger moments.

Let's slow the ride a moment. Stories like this remind us why we practiced—because one day, instinct will have to lead.

There's a story I think about often. It's not ancient or mythical—it happened right here, in the noise of a New York subway.

A young man had a seizure and fell onto the tracks. The train was already coming.
Another man, Wesley Autrey, saw it happen. He was standing there with his two daughters. No time to plan, no one shouting orders—just a moment of decision.

He jumped down.
He pressed the stranger flat into the trough between the rails and lay across him as the train roared above. When it stopped, both men were alive.
When reporters asked why he'd done it, Autrey said quietly, *"I just saw someone who needed help. I did what I felt was right."*

His daughters later said they weren't surprised. "Dad always helps," one told a reporter. There's something beautifully ordinary about that—heroism seen as a habit.

He didn't call himself a hero.
He didn't speak about fear or bravery.

He just acted as if saving another person were as ordinary as breathing.

That's what practice does.
When we live with compassion long enough, great things no longer seem extraordinary; they simply feel *natural*. Courage, kindness, mercy—they stop being choices we debate and become the rhythm of who we are.

It's the same truth we met back in *The Courage to Grow*—that strength ripens in small, consistent acts until it becomes character itself.

Maybe that's the secret we've been circling all along. When you practice love, *great things begin to feel like small things to do.*

The man on the subway didn't discover courage in that moment; he revealed it. It was already there, shaped quietly by a lifetime of care, small choices, and ordinary decency.

And that's how we all build it—not in moments of glory, but in the countless moments no one notices.

So if you ever wonder whether the little things matter—the small kindness, the gentle word, the patient pause—remember that man in the station, covered in dust but calm, saying, *"I did what I felt was right."*

That's what a life of practiced love looks like.
When the test comes, the heart doesn't hesitate.
It simply moves.

17. The Shadow Beside Us

The sky darkens faster than we expect. One moment, the road is silver with late light; the next, a curtain of gray rolls in from nowhere. A single drop strikes our arm—fat and cold. Then another. Then the heavens open all at once.

It isn't the soft kind of rain that smells like renewal. This one comes sideways—stinging, wild, angry with wind.

We pull over for a moment, watching it thrash the road ahead. The air smells of dust and metal. Thunder rolls somewhere behind the hills.
Strange how the world can change in a breath.

We've been riding together for a while now—through kindness and courage, through the quiet gentleness of love. But storms like this remind us there's another part of the road: the one where decency isn't easy, where the light fades, and where we begin to see what goodness looks like when it's tested.

Because love, as much as it warms the world, also casts a shadow.
And if we never look into that shadow, we'll never understand how easily the light can fade.

It's not a comfortable place.
But no moral journey is complete until we face the question that hums beneath every act of kindness: *what happens when people stop caring?*

We stand there a moment, hands on the handlebars, letting the rain sting our faces. Then we smile—just a little.
"Alright," we whisper to the storm. "Show us what you've got."

And we pedal forward into the rain.

The Reluctant Nazi
There's a story we can't ignore—not because it's grand, but because it's ordinary, and because it's true.

Once, long ago, there was a man—not a monster, not a fanatic—just a man who loved his family, paid his bills, and wanted to stay out of trouble. He'd been a teacher before the war. His students liked him. He believed in hard work, discipline, and order.

When the new party rose, he didn't cheer, but he didn't protest either.
He told himself it was politics, not his concern.

When the first new laws came, he grumbled quietly and filled out the forms. When his neighbors disappeared, he told himself it was probably for a reason. When the shop windows broke, he looked away.

Each step was small. Each compromise felt reasonable.

He wasn't a bad man—just a tired one, busy, worried about his job, hoping things would calm down.

Then one morning, he found himself at a desk, stamping papers that decided who could travel and who could not. He didn't know where those trains went, not exactly.
But he suspected.

And when the war ended, and the cameras came, and the world asked him *why*, he said the same thing we've all heard before:

"I was only doing my job."

It's easy to shake our heads now, to say, "We'd never do that."
But that's what he said once, too.

That's the thing about evil—it doesn't begin with hatred. It begins with silence.
With a shrug. With a quiet turning away.

It's hard to see the devil when his hand is on our shoulder.
He doesn't shout. He whispers.
He says, *"You're not responsible."*
He says, *"Everyone's doing it."*
He says, *"Stay out of it; keep your head down."*

And so good people drift.
Not because they choose darkness, but because they don't choose anything at all.

When we hear stories like this, we want to believe they belong to another time—another kind of person. But storms like this remind us: the rain may fall harder, but it's the same sky. The same human heart beneath it.

Each of us carries the capacity for light and for shadow.
And if we're honest, we know how easy it is to stop noticing when things get uncomfortable.

Maybe that's why we keep pedaling into the storm—to remember what it feels like when awareness stings, when the easy path washes away, and we have to choose which way to lean.

Let's take one breath here. The storm isn't only weather; it's perspective. Now watch what the next flash reveals.

The Banality of Evil

The rain doesn't let up.
It comes in sheets now, hammering the road until the line between sky and earth disappears. Every flash of lightning shows the world for what it is—bright for an instant, then gone again.

That's how evil often appears too—not as a monster in the shadows, but as the ordinary world caught in a brief, revealing light.

When Arendt wrote about the "banality of evil," she didn't mean wickedness is stupid; she meant it can *become ordinary*—what happens when people stop thinking about what they're doing. What she saw was far more unsettling: how evil becomes *ordinary* when people stop thinking about what they're doing.

144

The man on trial, Adolf Eichmann, wasn't a frothing villain. He was courteous, tidy, efficient. He didn't see himself as cruel; he saw himself as organized.
And that's the real danger. Evil doesn't need hatred — it only needs obedience.
The moment we stop asking questions, we become part of what we should have resisted.

Sometimes it isn't obedience at all. Sometimes it's distraction.
We get busy, tired, preoccupied. We tell ourselves, "I've got my own problems." We turn down the moral volume one notch at a time until silence feels normal.

A flash of lightning splits the clouds, and for a moment we can see everything — the road, the puddles, the trembling reflection of the sky. Then it's gone again. That's what thought does: it illuminates the landscape of conscience, even if just for a moment.

Arendt said Eichmann wasn't stupid; he was thoughtless.
That word stays with us. *Thoughtless*

Another gust slaps our jackets. The rain needles sideways again — brief, hard, clarifying.

Not evil in intention — just hollow.

And if we're honest, we know that space in ourselves. The days we drift through without noticing, when kindness costs effort and reflection feels like a luxury. Evil, it turns out, isn't always a presence. Sometimes it's an absence — the hollow space where empathy should have been.

145

That's the frightening part: how easy it is to drift there.
How routine can hide cruelty, and how even good systems can harm people if no one stops to look at who's being harmed.

We've all been in that moment. Watching someone scold a cashier, a stranger, a child—and doing nothing. Not because we wanted it to happen, but because we didn't want to get involved. And afterward, the quiet shame that settles in, the recognition that we were part of the silence.

No one is immune to that slide.
The shadow doesn't demand that we hate; it only asks that we stop noticing.

The rain softens now, tapping instead of thrashing. Maybe that's what storms are for—to wake us up.
To jolt us into awareness again, to make us feel.

Because once thought returns, empathy follows.
And that, more than outrage or blame, is what undoes the banality of evil: the simple act of *remembering what it feels like to care.*

As we ride on, we realize the storm isn't our enemy. Forgetting what clear air feels like—that's the real danger.

Experiments in Obedience
The storm deepens.
Thunder doesn't crash anymore—it rolls, slow and steady, like something that knows it will be heard. The rain turns heavy again, each drop striking with a kind of rhythm, like a drumbeat reminding us to pay attention.

We've been talking about how evil grows when people stop thinking.
But thoughtlessness doesn't always mean inaction.
Sometimes it looks like performance — people slipping into roles so completely they forget there's a person inside the part they're playing.

That's what happened in a basement at Stanford University, years ago, when a group of college students volunteered for a simple study on power and behavior. Half were assigned to be prisoners, half to be guards. It was meant to last two weeks. It barely lasted six days.

What happened down there is now infamous.
The guards were told only to "maintain order." That was it.
No script, no weapons, no real authority—just uniforms, sunglasses, and permission to enforce rules.

And yet, by the second day, the kindness began to leave their voices.
By the third, they were inventing punishments—push-ups, solitary confinement, public humiliation. The prisoners, stripped of names and given numbers, started to obey—not because they had to, but because they began to *believe* that they were less.

No one told them to be cruel.
No one said, "Forget these are your classmates."
The environment did that. The roles did that.

That's the most frightening truth the experiment revealed: we don't need violence to commit cruelty.
We only need *distance.*

147

The moment someone stops being a person and becomes "the other," almost anything becomes permissible.
A number. A label. A uniform.
Even kindness starts to sound like weakness.

And it doesn't take much to build that distance.
A word. A rule. A wall.
We've seen it in every chapter of history and every corner of daily life:
A child shunned for difference, a worker spoken to as a tool, a group defined by stereotype. Each small act of separation numbs the mind just enough to make empathy optional.

That's how dehumanization begins—not with hatred, but with language.
With jokes, nicknames, and paperwork. With small shifts in how we describe people until they no longer feel like "us."

And once that boundary is drawn, the rules of kindness no longer apply.
We stop saying "he" or "she." We start saying "they."
And then, "those people."
And finally, "it."

We stop saying "he" or "she." We start saying "they." And then something worse: we talk about people like problems to be managed. Language moves first; conscience follows—unless we notice and steer it back.

In the experiment, even the prisoners started to play along.
They began to forget who they were before the basement.

They followed their roles, obeyed rules they could have refused, and submitted to humiliation as though it were part of some moral order.

That's another truth we can't ignore: obedience isn't only about authority. It's also about belonging.

We crave acceptance so deeply that we'll sometimes surrender our conscience just to stay part of the group. We say what others say, do what others do, and call it morality because everyone around us agrees.

When the experiment ended, the students—both guards and prisoners—said they felt ashamed, confused, even haunted.

They hadn't known that such darkness was possible in them.

But that's the lesson, isn't it?

It doesn't take monsters. It takes *conditions*.

And those conditions are everywhere: in workplaces, in online spaces, in nations.

Anywhere empathy can be traded for role, uniform, or rule.

One of the psychologists watching from above finally called it off.

He realized he'd stopped seeing the students as people, too.

Even he had fallen into the script.

He'd become a scientist managing variables instead of a human watching suffering.

It's almost poetic, how the storm mirrors that realization.

We can't stay dry forever; eventually, the rain finds us.
Eventually, conscience seeps back in.

We like to believe we'd stand apart—that we'd be the ones to say, "This isn't right." But the experiment humbles us.
It whispers, *"You might not."*
And that humility is necessary.
Because moral strength doesn't come from believing we're incapable of cruelty.
It comes from knowing we are—and choosing differently.

What's astonishing is how quickly things healed when the roles ended.
Once the uniforms came off and the doors opened, the students embraced one another. Some even wept. The humanity they'd lost came rushing back, like air to lungs after being underwater.

That's the other side of the lesson: empathy, though fragile, is recoverable.
Even after darkness, we can remember who we are.

The rain softens again, but the world feels changed.
We know now how thin the line is between order and oppression, between rule and cruelty.

And so we ride on, quieter, more aware.
Because it isn't enough to say, "We'd never be like them."
We already are them—every one of us, capable of both the wound and the remedy.
The question isn't whether the storm exists.
It's whether we'll stay awake when the thunder fades.

The Fragility of Goodness

The storm drifts east, leaving behind a wet hush. The air feels emptied and clean, as though the world itself has paused to think.

We've seen how easily empathy can collapse—how ordinary people can lose sight of one another when fear, obedience, or distraction takes hold. But goodness, too, has its strange endurance. It bends, trembles, nearly disappears, yet never fully dies.

Even in the worst moments of history, someone always whispers, *"This isn't right."*
That quiet sentence — so small, yet so brave — is what we once called *the courage to act.*

There were farmers who hid families under their floors.
Nurses who smuggled medicine past soldiers.
Clerks who forged papers so that strangers could live.
A loaf of bread slipped through a fence.
A stranger's hand reaching for another's.

Each of these was the same moral instinct we once spoke of when we said compassion should reach beyond sight — the same spirit that moved us to help *the one we don't know.*
They were ordinary people extending care past their own safety, their own comfort, their own walls.

The smallest gestures carried moral weight beyond measure. They weren't enough to end the darkness—but they were enough to prove it hadn't won.

Goodness is fragile, but that fragility is what makes it sacred.

We often imagine virtue as armor, but it's more like glass—transparent, delicate, and easily broken. That doesn't make it weak. It makes it precious.

We know from experience how quickly kindness retreats. A sharp word, a cruel joke, a small humiliation—and suddenly goodness pulls back into silence. And yet, almost miraculously, it returns.
Someone asks, *"Are you alright?"*
Someone steps forward when no one else does.
And the world mends, if only by a thread.

Maybe the wonder of humanity isn't that we can be good, but that we *want* to be—even after seeing how much pain we cause.
That longing for decency, that hope in our better nature, is what we meant when we spoke of *honor*—not the pride of being right, but the dignity of trying to stay human.

In earlier chapters, we learned that love must be practiced to become real, that courage begins as trembling, and that compassion grows stronger the farther it reaches.
Now we see why all that mattered. Those lessons were never about feeling good—they were about surviving storms like this.

Goodness doesn't need to win; it only needs to endure.
Each time we choose awareness over apathy, patience over contempt, care over convenience, we keep it alive.

And that, perhaps, is the real measure of moral maturity: not how pure we become, but how persistently we return to kindness after forgetting it.

152

The air around us feels lighter now, washed of dust.
The road isn't bright yet, but we can see it again.
And for the moment, that's enough.

The Mirror of Conscience

When the storm finally moves on, there's that soft
stillness afterward — the kind that makes us pause.
We can almost hear the world breathing again.
It's in moments like this, after everything's been shaken,
that we catch our reflection.
Not the one we show to others, but the one that waits
behind the noise.

That's what conscience really is — a kind of mirror
we carry with us.
It doesn't shout or scold; it just reflects.
And it waits for us to look.

We spend a lot of time trying not to.
It's easier to stay busy, to keep our eyes on everyone else,
to measure the world instead of meeting our own gaze.
But when we finally stop — when the rush fades and the
quiet settles — there it is.
And if we're lucky, we look long enough to recognize
ourselves.

Have you ever felt that little tug, the one that comes
just before we speak sharply, or after we look away from
someone's need?
That's the mirror catching the light.
It doesn't accuse us; it just reminds us that we're still
capable of better.

We've walked a long road to reach this point.
We've seen how fear can drain compassion, how distance weakens empathy, how obedience dulls reflection.
But we've also seen that awareness changes everything —
the moment we notice, we begin to heal, and we remember what it means to care.

Maybe conscience isn't a burden at all.
Maybe it's the part of us that keeps the heart and mind in conversation.
The part that whispers, *"You can begin again."*

We've talked before about how love has to be practiced, how courage grows through small acts, how compassion expands only when we stretch it past comfort.
Now we can see why.
Each of those moments — every apology, every hesitation, every act of listening — is a way of polishing this mirror.

And what's reflected there isn't shame; it's possibility.
The same self that once turned away can turn back.
The same voice that went silent can speak.
The same hands that once did nothing can still do good.

Conscience doesn't promise perfection.
It promises awareness.
And awareness, when paired with care, is what keeps us human.

So maybe that's the quiet gift after the storm — not the certainty that we are good, but the trust that we can keep becoming so.

After the Storm

The road is quiet now.
The storm has passed, but its traces remain — puddles, branches, the faint smell of rain in the air.
We move slowly, not out of weariness but reverence.
Storms have a way of leaving us both unsettled and renewed.

Looking back, we can see how close goodness and danger travel.
How easy it is to drift from caring to compliance, from seeing to looking away.
We've walked beside ordinary people who lost their way, and others who found it again.
And maybe the hardest truth we've learned is that both kinds live within us.

Evil rarely appears as evil.
It sounds reasonable, efficient, professional.
It says, *"That's not your concern,"* or *"It's just the way things are."*
And we listen because it's easier than thinking, easier than feeling.

The tempter rarely looks like a villain; he sounds like common sense.
He doesn't tempt us to hate; he tempts us not to notice.
He calls our fear *prudence* and our silence *peace*.

That's why reflection matters so much — because awareness breaks the spell.
The moment we stop and think, the illusion cracks.
The moment we ask *why*, we begin to remember *who*.

All through this book, we've been practicing that kind of remembering.
Learning to listen before reacting.
To see before judging.
To care even when we don't have to.
Each chapter, in its own way, has been a rehearsal for conscience.

And now, as we stand in the clear air after the storm, we can see what it was all for.
Compassion isn't a feeling we wait for; it's a habit we choose.
Love isn't an accident of mood; it's a discipline of attention.
And morality isn't perfection; it's the courage to keep adjusting the course.

The rain has stopped.
The road shines ahead, washed clean but not erased.
There are still hills to climb, still shadows along the way.
But we know how to ride through them now — not with certainty, but with awareness.

Because the real work of goodness isn't to win against evil,
but to stay human while the storm passes over us.

18. The Morning After

The road remains slick, with puddles reflecting the pale morning light.
For the first time in a while, there's no thunder behind us—only the hush that comes after the world survives its own anger.

We stand still.
The bikes drip beside us; our clothes cling cold and heavy.
Water runs down our sleeves, each movement sending a shiver.
We're soaked through, but grateful to feel anything at all.

We don't cheer. We just breathe.
That's enough.

The world isn't perfect again.
Branches still block the path, and mud slicks the edges.
But everything glints a little, as if the light has been renewed.
We're not better—just more awake.
Maybe that's what goodness really is: the same world, seen with clearer eyes.

We talked once about a broken cup—how its cracks were filled with gold.
It's still with us, at least in memory, reminding us that

what breaks doesn't have to be hidden.
It can be honored.

Forgiveness works the same way.
The crack runs between us now, but we don't cover it.
We fill it with care.
Because healing isn't pretending it never shattered; it's loving what survived.

This morning feels like that—like the world has been stitched with Kintsugi seams, every crack lit by the returning sun.
Every wet leaf, every scar of the night shines a little golden.

We almost laugh—not from joy, but relief.
We made it through the storm without losing the will to be kind.

There's tenderness in the air, the kind that follows fright.
Our shoes squelch, our hands ache, but we still reach for one another out of simple gratitude.

And that's where goodness begins again—
not in grand gestures,
but in the quiet act of noticing.
That we're still here.
Together.

The Kindness That Follows Understanding
The first warmth of the morning doesn't come from the sun.
It comes from the small, uneasy laugh we share when we realize how soaked we still are.

It's not joy exactly, but relief.
Sometimes survival itself feels like grace.

After storms, something changes in us.
We start to notice small things again — the sound of
dripping water, the scent of earth, the simple fact that
we're still here.
And with that awareness comes a softer kind of strength.
It's not the loud courage that charges forward, but the
quiet one that bends down and begins to clean up.

That's often how compassion returns — not as a
grand vision, but as a small willingness to help.
We don't plan it or announce it.
We just do it.
Because once we've seen what harm looks like, we don't
want to add to it.

There's a word for this kind of mutual care: *Ubuntu.*
It means, "I am because we are."
It reminds us that humanity isn't an individual
achievement; it's something we maintain together.
When one person falls, we all feel the tremor.
When one person rises, we all stand a little taller.

For a long time, that idea sounded poetic but distant
— a beautiful phrase you might see printed on a poster or
spoken in a ceremony.
Now it feels less like poetry and more like physics.
Every life touches another.
Every word, every silence, every act carries outward,
sometimes in ways we'll never see.
We shape the weather around each other, for better or
worse.

159

We don't always notice it, but the most minor things we do change the temperature of the room — the way we speak to a clerk, the patience we give to a friend, the tone we take with a child.

Each moment is a chance to make the air warmer or colder.

That's what Ubuntu really means: we are the climate of one another's lives.

No one gets through life dry.
We depend on each other more than we like to admit.
And most of the good that keeps the world from falling apart happens quietly — in shared labor, in patience, in the everyday decision not to turn away.

Have you ever noticed how we remember the people who reached for us when we didn't have the words to ask?
Maybe kindness stays with us because it doesn't demand anything in return — it just shows up.

The Practice of Renewal
When the noise fades, there's always more to tend than we expect.
Putting things back in order, admitting what was neglected, finding the courage to begin again.
It isn't heroic work, but it's necessary.
That's how recovery begins — through small, steady acts of attention.

Moral renewal isn't about declaring that we've changed.
It's about returning, again and again, to the habits that

hold the world together: honesty, patience, restraint, and care.
After harm or indifference, goodness begins quietly, in gestures that could almost go unnoticed.

Philosophers call this kind of repair *moral work*.
It's the process of rebuilding trust — acknowledging harm, taking responsibility, and showing, through time, that we can do better.
It doesn't erase what happened.
It makes space for dignity to breathe again.

We've all had to do this kind of repair.
Sometimes it's between nations; sometimes it's between two people sitting across a table, both waiting for the other to speak first.
It starts with honesty.
A simple, difficult sentence: *"I know I hurt you."*
Or, just as brave: *"I'm ready to listen."*

That's where healing begins — not with forgiveness, not yet, but with recognition.
Before we can ask to be forgiven, we have to face what's true.
Before we can trust again, we have to make truth visible.
That's the groundwork of renewal.

It's not easy to face where we've fallen short.
But isn't it strange how much lighter we feel once we do?
There's a quiet relief that comes from honesty — like setting down something we didn't realize we'd been carrying.

One of the wisest pieces of advice I've ever come across was from Stephen Covey's *The Seven Habits of*

161

Highly Effective People:
"Seek first to understand, then to be understood."
It sounds simple, but it's revolutionary in practice.
To understand someone before defending ourselves — to
listen without waiting for our turn to speak — is one of
the purest forms of compassion.
It quiets pride and opens space for repair.
Most broken bonds aren't healed by argument; they're
mended by listening.

Moral repair doesn't always look noble from the
outside; sometimes it looks like two ordinary people
trying not to talk over each other.

I think about this every time Darla and I have one of
those small household *"debates"* — the kind every couple
has.
You know the moment: both of us talking, both certain the
other isn't listening.
In my head, I'm thinking, *"Why can't she hear what I'm
saying?"*
And I'd bet she's thinking the same thing about me.
The truth is, she's one of the best listeners I know — me
not so much — so it's only half true, but the story still fits.
The moment one of us stops trying to win and starts
listening, everything softens.
It's the same at home, at work, anywhere people care
about each other.
Most conflicts aren't about who's right — they're about
who's willing to listen first.

What's remarkable is how often this works.
Whole communities have been rebuilt on nothing more
than people telling the truth and staying to hear it.

Families mend that way.
Friendships too.
When we repair something moral, the crack never disappears — but it becomes the place where light gets in.

Renewal asks for both courage and compassion.
It isn't a single act; it's a discipline.
It's the daily decision to move toward the better thing, even when the memory of failure still clings.
Over time, that decision becomes a kind of moral muscle.
Each repetition strengthens our capacity for decency.

Renewal doesn't make us spotless; it makes us steady.
It's not about perfection but persistence — the quiet promise that we will keep trying to do right by one another.
That's how trust is restored.
That's how conscience becomes habit again.

The Bridge Between Seeing and Doing

We've all had that feeling — the quiet voice inside that says, *"Do something,"* right before we hesitate.
We see what needs to be done, but the doing takes a little longer to catch up.
That space between knowing and acting is where most of life's struggle happens.

We all know that gap.
Have you ever sat with a thought — knowing it was right — and still waited, hoping someone else would move first?
We call it hesitation, but most of the time it's just fear wearing better manners.

Knowing what's right doesn't make it easy.
Even when our hearts are in the right place, the body still resists.
We worry about saying the wrong thing, stepping out of line, or just getting too tired.
And yet, that's exactly where compassion lives — in the moments when we act anyway.

We've talked before about how love isn't just something we feel; it's something we practice.
The same is true for kindness, courage, patience — all the things that make life gentler.
They don't grow in silence; they grow in motion.
Every time we show up, even a little, we're shaping who we are.

When we start to live by what we understand, the world starts to open back up.
We begin to see the person behind the argument, the worry behind the anger, the hope behind the stubbornness.
It's hard to be cruel when we're truly paying attention.
And once we see someone clearly, indifference doesn't stand a chance.

We don't need to be perfect at it.
Half the time, we stumble through.
But we keep trying — together.
That's the bridge between seeing and doing: not perfection, but persistence.
The quiet effort to live what we know, even when we're still learning how.

Sometimes we forget that moral life isn't a solo climb. It's a shared path.
We learn by example, by encouragement, by seeing goodness in someone else and realizing, *"I could do that too."*
And when we fail — which we all do — we begin again, a little humbler, a little wiser, and hopefully, a little kinder.

Every time we cross that bridge — from thought to action, from understanding to care — it gets easier to find our way back.
That's how goodness grows: one small step at a time, together.

The Terrain of Becoming
When we look back, it's hard to say exactly when things began to shift.
Maybe it was the first time we noticed how much effort it takes to stay kind.
Or maybe it was when we realized that understanding someone doesn't come from agreeing with them, but from truly hearing them.
Whatever it was, something has settled in us — a steadiness that wasn't there before.

We've learned that compassion isn't an emotion we wait for; it's a way of moving through the world.
It grows from practice, from all the small moments when we choose patience over pride, curiosity over certainty.
We don't need grand gestures.
Just the quiet discipline of showing up, even when no one's watching.

And somewhere along the way, we began to see that love is not a single feeling but a habit of attention.
It's in the way we pause before judging, the way we forgive someone who doesn't ask, the way we keep trying even when it's inconvenient.
We start to recognize that every act of care — however small — pushes back against the indifference that creeps into the world.

It's funny how moral life looks less like a map and more like a landscape: hills and valleys, moments of clarity followed by fog.
But even when we stumble, we know the direction now.

Have you noticed how the same lessons begin to sound different once you've lived them for a while?
It's not that we learn new truths — we just start believing the old ones more deeply.

Sometimes I think the point of all this isn't to arrive somewhere perfect, but to stay awake along the way.
To keep noticing.
To keep choosing.
To keep practicing until goodness feels less like a decision and more like a reflex.

And maybe that's what growing wiser really means: needing fewer reasons to be kind.

The Morning Road
The air feels lighter now.
Not bright exactly, but open — like a door left ajar after a long night.
We stand for a moment, not to admire the view, but just

to feel that we can.
Everything is still damp, but it no longer feels heavy.

When we begin to move again, there's no hurry in our steps.
The world is ordinary — puddles, birds, the hum of a distant engine — but ordinary feels like a blessing.
We don't talk much.
There's a quiet understanding between us, the kind that doesn't need words.

We've been through enough together to know that the road doesn't promise ease.
But there's comfort in knowing that when we lose our way, we can begin again.
We've learned that goodness doesn't depend on perfect conditions — it depends on the steady work of our hearts.

Maybe that's what all of this has been teaching us — that renewal isn't something that happens *after* the hard part; it happens *through* it.
The world doesn't hand us light; we keep passing it forward.

I don't think we'll ever stop stumbling.
But each time we rise, we do it with a little more care.
Maybe that's all renewal really asks of us: to keep trying, to keep mending, to keep moving toward what's better.

As the light grows, the world takes on that soft, golden look that comes just after rain.
We don't need to say anything profound.
It's enough to know that we've made it this far, together.

Up ahead, the road bends toward town.
Somewhere beyond that turn, there will be new mistakes,

new lessons, new chances to make things right.
And soon — perhaps sooner than we expect — we'll talk
about forgiveness.
For now, it's enough to walk in quiet company,
feeling the world warm again beneath us.

19. The Measure of Forgiveness

Could you ever forgive someone who had taken the life of a friend or a family member?
Most of us would say no — at least, not right away, maybe not ever.
I don't know if I could either.
It feels important to start there — with honesty.
It's easy to talk about compassion in theory, but forgiveness asks something deeper.
It asks us to let go when everything in us wants to hold on.
And if we're honest, most of us don't know how far our mercy reaches until it's tested.
I hope I never have to find out.
But I'm grateful to know that such grace exists in the world — proof that goodness can still rise even from ruin.
It gives us something to reach for, and to pray we never need.

A few years ago, a man walked into a small church in Charleston, South Carolina.
He joined the congregation for their Wednesday-night Bible study.
He bowed his head as they prayed together, spoke with them as friends — and then, moments later, opened fire.

Nine people were killed, including the pastor who had welcomed him in.

Days later, during his hearing, the families of those victims stood in front of him.
And one by one, they forgave him.
They said things like, *"You took something precious from me, but I forgive you,"* and *"May God have mercy on your soul."*

For a long moment after hearing those words, I couldn't move. Even now, thinking about them, I feel the same stillness—the quiet disbelief that such mercy could exist in the same world as that harm.

There was no anger in their voices, only sorrow and an astonishing calm.

When I first heard those words, I didn't know what to make of them.
It felt almost impossible — superhuman.
How do you forgive someone who has done that?
But that moment reminded us that forgiveness isn't about erasing pain or pretending evil didn't happen.
It's about refusing to let hate be the final word.
Those families stood where most of us could not — and somehow, they found compassion in the rubble.

Not long after, another act of grace emerged in Boston.
A man who lost his leg in the marathon bombing publicly forgave the attackers.
He said that anger would only destroy what they couldn't.
I remember thinking: how do you say that, after what you've been through?

But maybe he understood something we forget — that forgiveness is a form of self-preservation.
It doesn't excuse evil; it releases us from carrying it.

And then, a quieter story — one that didn't fill headlines for long, but lingered in the hearts of those who heard it.
In Texas, an off-duty police officer entered the wrong apartment and killed **Botham Jean**, an innocent man relaxing in his own home.
At the sentencing, his brother, **Brandt Jean,** asked to speak.
He turned to the woman who had taken his brother's life and said, *"I forgive you."*
Then he stepped forward and hugged her.
He didn't do it to make a statement; he did it because something in him couldn't live with hatred.

I still think about that moment.
I don't know if I could have done the same.
Maybe you've wondered that too — what would I do if it were me?
Would I have that kind of strength?
Forgiveness, when we see it up close, isn't gentle or easy.
It's raw, trembling, human.
But it's also one of the few things that can stop the chain of pain from continuing.

Have you ever noticed how stories like these stay with us?
They remind us that goodness doesn't vanish just because cruelty shows up.
Forgiveness is a light we can't always hold, but we can still see it — and seeing it changes us.

171

It shows us what we could be, even when we're not there yet.

The Weight of the Wound

Forgiveness sounds noble until you're the one asked to give it.

Then it becomes something else — heavier, slower, almost unreasonable.

We tell ourselves that time heals all wounds, but what time really does is give the wound more room to speak.

And it speaks in strange ways: anger, silence, fear, pride, exhaustion.

It's not that we don't want to forgive — it's that part of us still needs the world to know what was taken.

There's a reason forgiveness feels so unnatural.

It pushes against one of our oldest instincts — the need for justice.

When someone hurts us, something in us demands balance.

We want the scales set right.

We want acknowledgment, punishment, maybe even revenge.

To forgive can feel like betrayal — like letting go of the only proof that what happened *mattered.*

But here's the quiet truth: holding onto pain doesn't preserve meaning; it multiplies suffering.

It's like clutching a burning coal to prove we've been burned. The longer we hold it, the more it scars the hand that refuses to let go.

And yet — we all do it.

Maybe because anger feels safer than grief.

Anger keeps us standing, while grief brings us to our knees.

If you've ever tried to forgive before you were ready, you know how hollow it feels.
We can't force the heart to open just because the mind says it should.
Forgiveness isn't a decision we make once; it's a process we keep meeting.
Sometimes it begins not with release, but with honesty: *I'm not there yet, but I want to be.*

Have you ever noticed how forgiveness doesn't start with the offender at all?
It starts with us — with the way we carry pain.
At some point, we grow tired of the weight.
We realize that our anger, once protective, has begun to own us.
That's when forgiveness starts to whisper, not as mercy for them, but as mercy for ourselves.

The people in Charleston, Boston, and Texas didn't forgive because it was easy or expected.
They forgave because they refused to live chained to the moment that hurt them.
That's the quiet power of forgiveness — it doesn't erase the past; it frees the future.

The Turning Point
There comes a moment — not loud or dramatic — when something inside us begins to soften.
The anger that once felt like armor starts to feel like a burden.

We don't plan it; it just happens.
A thought, a memory, a face — and suddenly the sharp
edges dull just enough for us to breathe again.

Forgiveness rarely begins with a grand declaration.
It starts in smaller places:
The quiet realization that we don't want to rehearse the
pain anymore,
the tiredness that comes from carrying the same story,
the first hint that peace might be worth more than pride.

Sometimes it feels almost unfair, this turning.
We spent so long defending our pain — we built whole
walls around it — and now it begins to crumble, not
because it stopped mattering, but because we've grown
too large to live inside it.
It's humbling when you realize that you can't heal and
hold resentment at the same time.

We've spoken before about how growth often begins
in noticing.
Forgiveness is no different.
It doesn't ask us to forget or excuse, only to see that our
hurt has begun to own us.
The moment we notice that, something opens.
Not much, just a crack wide enough for light to find its
way in.

Have you ever found yourself remembering someone
who hurt you and, for the first time, not feeling angry —
just sad?
That sadness is often the doorway.
It's where the wound turns from a weapon into a scar.

It doesn't mean we've excused them.
It means we've begun to reclaim ourselves.

Forgiveness doesn't make the past right; it makes the future possible.
It says: *What you did was wrong, but it won't be the end of me.*
And in that defiance, there's freedom.
It's not a weakness.
Its strength returning in its gentlest form.

Sometimes I think of it like unclenching a fist.
At first, the hand resists — the muscles ache from holding tight for so long.
But the longer we stay open, the easier it becomes to hold nothing and still feel whole.

Forgiveness doesn't erase the story.
It changes the way we carry it.
And that change — small, almost invisible at first — is the turning point where healing begins.

The Courage to Let Go
There's a moment in every healing where we face a choice:
To keep carrying the wound, or to let it rest.
Letting go sounds simple, but it's one of the bravest things a person can do.
It means living without the story that's protected us, without the anger that's made us feel strong.

We don't talk enough about how much courage forgiveness takes.
It's not the absence of pain — it's the decision to keep loving life in spite of it.

That's why it feels like such a climb.
Every step upward means setting down a piece of pride, a piece of fear, a piece of certainty that we were right and they were wrong.
Forgiveness doesn't erase what happened; it erases the claim it has on our future.

And it takes time — more than we like to admit.
Sometimes we think we've forgiven, only to feel the anger spark again when we remember the details.
That's not failure; that's the heart doing its slow, stubborn work.
We have to forgive more than once, sometimes for the same thing, before the hurt finally loosens its grip.

Have you ever felt how heavy anger sits in the body?
The clenched jaw, the tight shoulders, the way sleep never comes easy?
Letting go isn't abstract — it's physical.
You feel the difference when you release it.
The chest opens.
The breath deepens.
It's as if the body finally believes what the soul's been trying to say: *You're safe now.*

Forgiveness is rarely witnessed.
No one throws a parade when we finally stop hating someone.
No one even knows it happened.
But inside, everything shifts.
The room grows lighter.
The world feels wide again.

We used to think of strength as holding on to power, to pain, to principle.
But the real strength is knowing when to set something down.
That's what forgiveness is: the quiet courage to unclench our hearts.

From One Heart to Many

Forgiveness begins quietly, inside a single life.
But once we learn what it costs—and what it gives—we start to see it everywhere.
What one person does in private, a community can do in public.
The same moral motion that softens one heart can, in time, heal a nation.

We've felt what it takes to let go of a single wrong.
Now imagine doing that with an entire history.
Imagine facing not one wound, but generations of them— and still choosing reconciliation over revenge.
That's what Desmond Tutu asked of his country, and of us all.

The Grace That Heals Nations

When South Africa emerged from apartheid, the air was thick with bitterness.
Whole communities had been torn apart.
Every family carried a story of loss — a son disappeared, a mother humiliated, a father beaten.
Justice demanded punishment.
But Archbishop Desmond Tutu believed that punishment

177

alone couldn't build a future.
He believed the truth had to be spoken, but also that it had to be heard with the intention to heal.

So he helped create something the world had never seen before — the *Truth and Reconciliation Commission*.
People came forward to tell what they had done and what had been done to them.
There were tears, silence, and sometimes shouting.
There were faces bowed in shame, and others lifted in unbearable pain.
And through it all, Tutu sat at the center, listening.
Not as a judge, but as a witness.

He wept often — so much that his handkerchief became as symbolic as his purple robes.
Some called him naïve for believing that people could change.
But he never mistook forgiveness for forgetfulness.
He said, *"Forgiving is not forgetting; it's remembering and not using your right to hit back."*
That small difference — between denial and release — is what made his vision work.

When a mother told the Commission how her child had been murdered, she spoke not only to condemn, but to reclaim her dignity.
When a soldier confessed his crimes, he did not undo the past, but he reopened the possibility of being human again.
Each act of truth-telling was a form of moral surgery — cutting deep, but meant to heal.

We often imagine forgiveness as a soft thing —
delicate, saintly, even weak.
But watching Tutu, you realized it was made of steel. We
felt that steel, even from afar — the steady courage that
invites us to believe human hearts can still turn toward
one another.
It took more strength to keep the heart open than to close
it.
And in the end, the power of the Commission wasn't that
everyone forgave — it was that everyone was finally seen.

Maybe that's what forgiveness really is: a kind of
seeing.
To look at what was done and still say, *You no longer
control me.*
That's freedom, the kind that nations and people both
hunger for.

Tutu once said, *"Without forgiveness, there is no future."*
He didn't mean it as poetry — he meant it as survival.
Because the only way to break the chain of cruelty is for
someone to stop pulling.
Someone has to choose to be the ending instead of the
echo.

And that's what those families in Charleston did.
It's what survivors in Boston and Texas did.
It's what Tutu asked of his country — and what, in
quieter ways, life keeps asking of all of us.

The Freedom That Remains
Forgiveness doesn't always make the world fair
again, but it makes it livable.

It gives us a way to keep walking through the wreckage without becoming part of it.

There's a kind of freedom that remains after forgiveness — not the freedom to forget, but the freedom to begin again.

I think of John Lewis when I think of that kind of courage.

After being beaten on the Edmund Pettus Bridge, he carried the scars for the rest of his life — physical reminders of how cruel the world can be.

And yet, when asked about the men who had attacked him, he said he forgave them.

Years later, one of them came to him in tears to apologize, and Lewis embraced him.

He said, *"We all have to be reconciled."*

That's not weakness.

That's the deepest kind of power — to turn pain into bridgework.

We've seen that power in Tutu, in the families of Charleston, in survivors of Boston and Texas — and maybe, in quieter ways, in ourselves.

Each of them shows that forgiveness isn't the end of justice; it's the continuation of love.

It doesn't erase what happened.

It says, *You don't get to decide what I become.*

Have you ever noticed how people who forgive seem lighter, even when they've endured more than most of us could bear?

Maybe that's because forgiveness is the only thing strong enough to unburden the soul.

It doesn't change the past, but it transforms our

relationship to it.
And once we stop feeding the darkness, something else begins to grow.

There's a quiet peace in that — not triumph, not closure, just peace.
The kind that allows us to breathe without bitterness.
The kind that turns a wound into a scar, and a scar into a story worth telling.

Forgiveness doesn't make us saints.
It makes us human again.
It's the choice to live as though the future still matters.
And maybe that's the truest freedom of all — the freedom to love again, even after everything.

20. The Shared Language of the Sacred

The morning feels washed clean.
The streets are still damp, and sunlight glints off puddles like tiny mirrors.
As we pass through town, there's a calm you can almost feel — the kind that makes you notice what's always been there but too easy to miss.

A church bell rings somewhere behind us.
A few blocks ahead, the call to prayer drifts softly from a mosque.
Farther on, a temple door stands open, the air scented with incense and quiet chanting.
Different doors, same invitation: to come in, to reflect, to remember what matters.

From the outside, they look nothing alike — domes and crosses, candles and carpets — yet each holds a circle of people trying to live good lives.
To love, to forgive, to tell the truth, to care for one another.
Different languages, same message.

If we listen closely, we can hear the harmony that runs beneath them all — a rhythm older than any scripture:
Be kind. Do no harm. Help when you can.

Maybe holiness isn't about believing the same thing, but about remembering that we belong to one another.

We've spent these chapters tracing compassion from the personal to the public.
Now we turn to the moral maps that guided humanity long before us — the sacred blueprints for living decently with one another, whatever name we give the divine.

The Ancient Roots of Guidance
Long before philosophy or psychology gave us words like *ethics* and *empathy*, people were already asking the same questions we ask now:
How should we live?
What keeps us from tearing one another apart?
How do we make life fair, or at least bearable?

The earliest answers came as stories and laws, carved in stone or passed by firelight.
They weren't meant to crush freedom — they were meant to protect it.
The _Ten Commandments_, for instance, sound stern when read aloud, but beneath each "Thou shalt not" lives a quiet promise: *if you keep these, we can trust each other.*
"Do not steal" means you can sleep without fear.
"Do not bear false witness" means your name is safe when you're not in the room.
They weren't just divine decrees — they were blueprints for peace.

Later came the _Seven Virtues_, the other side of that same coin — not prohibitions, but aspirations.
Courage, justice, prudence, temperance, faith, hope, and charity.

183

If the Commandments taught us what not to do, the Virtues whispered what we might become.

They were habits of heart — the moral equivalent of muscles that grow stronger with use.

As we've said before, love and compassion aren't talents; they're practiced strengths.

And then there are the _Beatitudes,_ soft where the Commandments are firm.

"Blessed are the merciful."

"Blessed are the peacemakers."

"Blessed are the pure in heart."

They don't warn or threaten; they invite.

They speak to the spirit of the law rather than the letter of it — not about punishment, but about potential.

Each one is a reminder that gentleness, too, is a form of strength.

Across centuries, these teachings were less about obedience than about balance.

They weren't lists to memorize, but maps for how to live among others without losing ourselves.

You can hear the same music behind them that we've followed all along:

Love your neighbor. Be just. Forgive. Begin again.

The Eastern Paths of Compassion

If we travel a little farther in our thoughts, the scenery changes—but the questions remain the same.

Far from the deserts and chapels of the West, other voices were asking what it means to live well, to suffer wisely, to care deeply.

Their answers, though spoken in different languages, sound like replies to the same ancient call.

In _Buddhism,_ morality begins not with sin but with suffering — the recognition that life brings pain, and that compassion is the way through it.
The _Eightfold Path_ is less a set of commandments than a way of walking: _right view, right speech, right action._
It asks us to live awake, to speak truthfully, to act with care.
Not because we fear punishment, but because mindfulness itself is mercy — a kind of attention that keeps us from doing harm.
It's a morality of awareness, reminding us that every thought and gesture ripples outward.

In _Hinduism,_ goodness is expressed through _dharma_ — living in harmony with what's true, fulfilling our duties without clinging to reward.
It's the bow of the yogi, hands pressed together, head lowered — a gesture that means, _The divine in me honors the divine in you._
That's not poetry; it's worldview.
It's saying, "You and I are made of the same light."
When we forget that, cruelty grows easy.
When we remember, compassion feels natural again.

And in _Confucianism_, morality is not about gods or heavens, but about relationships.
Respect between parent and child, friend and friend, leader and citizen.
Confucius believed that virtue begins in the smallest gestures — a bow, a tone of voice, a kindness extended to a stranger.

185

To him, harmony wasn't something we waited for; it was something we practiced every day.
Kindness wasn't weakness, but social glue.

If we pause here, among these teachings, we can feel the rhythm repeating:
Compassion. Duty. Awareness. Respect.
Whether carved in stone or written on rice paper, the lessons point in the same direction.
We are not islands.
We are threads — and when we move gently, the whole fabric holds.

The Prophets of Renewal

Every age seems to bring its own prophets — not the kind who predict the future, but the kind who remind us what we've forgotten.
They rise from pulpits, prisons, classrooms, and street corners, carrying the same message in new hands: that love is strength, that mercy is power, that justice without compassion turns cruel.

We've met some of them before — Desmond Tutu, whose laughter sounded like sunlight even after years of darkness.
His call for forgiveness wasn't meant to make the past disappear; it was meant to give the future a chance to exist.
His words — *"Without forgiveness, there is no future"* — still ring beneath history like a tuning fork for the human soul.

And then there was *Martin Luther King Jr.*, who believed love could be a weapon sharper than hate.

He once said, *"Love is the only force capable of transforming an enemy into a friend."*
Those weren't words from a comfortable man; they were spoken by someone who had seen the cost of peace.
King didn't ask us to be passive; he asked us to be powerful in a different way — to meet injustice without becoming it.

The *Dalai Lama* carries that same thread through a gentler fabric.
He teaches compassion not as charity, but as survival — that if others suffer, so will we.
He reminds us to see everyone as kin, perhaps even as family from another lifetime.
Even if we don't share his belief in rebirth, we can still feel the wisdom in it: that the stranger you help today might once have been the one who helped you.

And for those who seek goodness without religion, there's *Humanism*, which finds the sacred in the simple fact of being alive together.
Its tenets ask no faith but the faith in decency — to think clearly, to act kindly, to take responsibility for one another because there is no one else to do it.
Humanism says that morality is not handed down from the sky but grows from the heart.
In that sense, it's not opposed to faith at all — it's faith turned inward, trusting that humanity itself is capable of goodness.

Different robes, same spirit.
Each of these voices, in its own way, echoes what we've been hearing since the beginning:
That compassion is not an ornament of life but its

purpose.
That truth and mercy are two sides of the same coin,
and that the measure of any belief — sacred or secular —
is how it treats the vulnerable.

If we listen closely, these teachers aren't competing.
They're harmonizing.
They remind us that moral renewal isn't something
history gives us; it's something we must keep choosing,
again and again.

The Common Thread

If you strip away the rituals and languages, the names
of gods and saints, what remains is a single idea that
seems to appear wherever people have tried to live
together:
Treat others as you wish to be treated.

It's carved into stone tablets and written in the
margins of holy books.
It's whispered by monks, sung in choirs, chanted in
temples, and printed on classroom walls.
The *Golden Rule* — or something like it — exists in nearly
every tradition humanity has ever built.

In *Christianity*, it's spoken plainly: *"Do unto others as
you would have them do unto you."*
In *Judaism*, it's phrased as restraint: *"What is hateful to you,
do not do to your neighbor."*
In *Islam*, it's a reminder of empathy: *"None of you truly
believes until he loves for his brother what he loves for himself."*
In *Buddhism*, it becomes compassion without self: *"Hurt
not others in ways that you yourself would find hurtful."*

188

And in *Humanism*, the same thought is written without heaven or hell — simply: *"We are responsible for one another."*

We might disagree on nearly everything else, but this — this we share.
It's as if the human heart, wherever it beats, keeps arriving at the same conclusion.
That we survive by caring, that we grow by giving, that dignity is not a reward but a right.

Maybe that's what morality really is — not divine command, not cultural inheritance, but the recognition of shared fragility.
We all need help.
We all fear loss.
We all hope to be understood.
And so we build these mirrors of kindness, generation after generation, to remind us who we are when we forget.

If you've ever seen a child help another without being told, or an elder share food with someone they barely know, you've seen this rule alive.
It doesn't require translation, only attention.
It's the grammar of goodness, the syntax of care.
And when we practice it — at home, at work, in the ordinary corners of our days — we add our verse to the same long song that's been sung since the beginning.

The Sacred as Practice

The Golden Rule has carried us a long way — a bridge between faiths, philosophies, and generations.

But like any old bridge, it creaks under the weight of time. "Do unto others as you would have them do unto you" is a beautiful start, but life keeps teaching us that goodness must stretch further.

What if what I want isn't what you need?
What if my comfort feels like pressure to you?
What if my way of showing care is the very thing that makes you turn away?
Love that begins with "I" can still be blind.

Compassion grows deeper when it becomes less about *I* and more about *we*.
Not "Do unto others as I would want," but "Do unto others as *they* would want — because we are in this together."
That shift — from empathy to understanding — is what turns kindness into wisdom.

We've touched this truth before: in Singer's call to help the unseen, in Noddings's idea of the *carer and cared-for*, in our own stumbles toward listening before speaking. Goodness isn't a single act; it's a relationship.
It means learning to see through another's eyes without needing their world to look like ours.

If we're honest, that's hard.
It asks for patience, humility, and the willingness to be uncomfortable.
But it's also where love becomes real — where compassion stops being an idea and becomes a practice.

Maybe that's what holiness looks like now: not certainty, not agreement, but attention.
The way we show up for one another, even when it's

inconvenient.
The way we keep trying to understand what another
heart needs, even when it doesn't match our own.

If the world is a cathedral, its stained glass isn't made
of doctrine — it's made of moments like these:
a kindness offered at the right time,
a word held back when anger burns,
a small act of care that no one will ever see.

That's the sacred made visible — not in stone or
scripture, but in us.
When we live with that awareness, every place becomes
holy ground.
And maybe that's what the Golden Rule was always
trying to say — not *do unto others as you would have them do
unto you,*
but *remember: there is no you without us.*

21. The Wires We Reach For

In the 1950s, a psychologist named Harry Harlow tried to answer a question most of us assume we already know: *Why do we need love?*

He raised baby rhesus macaques with two mothers — one made of wire, one covered in soft cloth.
The wire mother held a bottle of milk.
The cloth mother offered nothing but warmth.
Logic said the infants would cling to the one who fed them.
But Harlow watched as the babies wrapped their arms around the cloth mother instead, holding tight even when hungry.
They would dart to the wire one for food, then hurry back to the soft one for safety.

He once described a frightened infant pressed against its cloth mother as "quivering, clinging, and silent."
It was heartbreaking and tender at the same time — proof that nourishment alone isn't enough.
We don't survive on food; we survive on comfort.

When we think about it, that little monkey is all of us at some point.
Maybe not in a cage, but clinging to something that feels safe — a voice, a hand, a familiar face.

We reach for warmth before we reach for reason.
Isn't it strange how often we forget that?

Many of us can name our own "cloth mother" in life
— a person, a memory, a ritual, even a pet.
Something that tells the nervous system, *You're okay. You can rest now.*
We all have one, whether we admit it or not.
And we all have a few wire ones too — the things we mistake for comfort: busyness, control, approval.
We keep returning to them, even though they never really make us feel better.
(That part usually earns a knowing smile — we've all hugged a wire mother or two.)

Harlow wasn't studying cruelty; he was trying to measure love in a language science could understand.
And in doing so, he gave us something philosophy and religion had been saying for centuries — that affection is not decoration; it's foundation.
Without it, everything else in us starts to fray.

When someone truly listens, the whole body exhales.
That's the same need the baby monkey showed, just grown taller and wearing shoes.
We never outgrow the desire to feel safe in someone's arms — even if now those arms are made of trust, kindness, or understanding.

Maybe that's the quiet truth behind Harlow's work — that the soul, like the body, needs holding.
And the greatest proof of our humanity might be that we reach not only to be held, but to hold back.

The First Lesson of the Heart

Long before we learn words like *right* and *wrong*, we learn *safe* and *unsafe*.

Before we ever say "I love you," we learn what love feels like — or what its absence feels like.

That first lesson becomes the quiet foundation beneath every moral choice we'll ever make.

Psychologists now call it *attachment theory*.
But parents, grandparents, and anyone who's ever soothed a crying child already know it by instinct.
A child learns trust when a need is met — hunger answered, fear comforted, loneliness held.
That's the beginning of empathy: realizing that comfort can be given, not just received.

It's strange how much of our adult life still circles that same lesson.
We tell ourselves we've grown up, become rational, independent, self-sufficient — and yet, one kind word can still undo us, can't it?
One voice saying, *We see you, you're not alone,* and suddenly the world feels less sharp around the edges.

Sometimes it seems morality begins right there — in the moment we realize that what soothes us can soothe someone else.
It's not grand philosophy; it's memory.
The body remembers what comfort feels like, and the heart simply imitates it outward.

When that foundation is strong, compassion comes easily.
When it's cracked — through neglect, fear, or cruelty —

we spend years trying to rebuild it.
We can almost feel it in one another.
Some of us move through life like open hands.
Others move like we're still braced for impact.

And who can blame us?
When love was scarce or unpredictable, self-protection
became the only way to feel safe.
We all build our armor from the materials we were given.

But the remarkable thing about being human —
maybe our saving grace — is that we can learn warmth
later.
We can be held by friendship, by faith, by community, by
kindness from strangers.
And in time, even those of us who grew up among wire
can learn what cloth feels like.

We've seen how people who offer comfort most easily
are often the ones who went without it.
Perhaps we learned the hard way how much it matters.
Perhaps we made a promise, even silently, never to let
anyone else feel that cold.

We've spoken throughout this book about
compassion as strength.
This is where it begins — in the quiet exchange between
need and care, between fear and reassurance.
The first moral law, older than any commandment, might
simply be this:
When we see trembling, we reach out our hand.

The Wires We Carry

We may outgrow our cribs, but we never quite stop reaching for comfort.

The only difference is that, as adults, our "mothers" look different.

Some of them are made of success, others of attention, others of glowing screens that promise connection but leave us lonelier than before.

If Harlow's monkeys reach for wire and cloth, we reach for approval and distraction — anything that feels like safety for a little while.

It's easy to smile at that.

We all have our "wire mothers" — the things that keep us busy, important, or distracted, but never really warm.

Some of us wrap ourselves in overwork, some in pride, some in always needing to be right.

They're familiar, shiny, dependable — and utterly incapable of love.

What's strange is how hard it is to tell the difference.

We can chase achievement or control or attention for years before we realize they never quite feed the part of us that's hungry.

We eat, but we don't feel full.

We win, but we don't feel safe.

There's nothing wrong with wanting success or structure.

But comfort that asks us to earn it isn't comfort — it's a transaction.

We all fall for that trap now and then: mistaking what quiets the noise for what heals the ache.

If we look closely, we can see it in our habits.
We scroll when we should rest.
We lecture when we should listen.
We retreat when someone reaches for us.
Maybe that's just the nervous system remembering an old lesson — that wire feels safer than risk.

It takes practice to recognize what real warmth feels like again.
And it usually arrives in small, ordinary moments:
someone remembering our name,
a laugh shared at the right time,
a silence that doesn't need to be filled.
That's what cloth feels like.

We don't always notice it right away, but those are the moments that rewire us — the simple human gestures that remind the frightened parts of us that it's okay to trust again.

We've learned by now how many cruelties begin simply because someone forgot what comfort feels like. We can spend our whole lives chasing substitutes for love, but nothing we invent works quite as well as the real thing.

Maybe the work of compassion, then, is learning to tell the difference — to stop settling for wire when what we really need is warmth.
And maybe, if we can do that for ourselves, we'll start doing it for one another too.

The Science of Warmth

Science has a funny way of proving what the heart already knows.
We used to think kindness was something we learned — a rule, a choice, a virtue we reached for.
But the more we study ourselves, the more it looks like we were born that way.

Our bodies tell the story better than any sermon.
When we're held, our pulse steadies.
When we laugh, our brain releases oxytocin — the same little spark that bonds a newborn to its mother.
Even a friendly hand on the shoulder can lower blood pressure.
We may call it compassion, but nature calls it maintenance.

We're built for connection.
Every shared meal, every good laugh, every comforting word lights up the same parts of the brain that tell us we're safe.
We don't just *enjoy* kindness — we *depend* on it.
It keeps our hearts from racing too fast, our fears from talking too loudly.

It makes us smile to think that love, for all its mystery, is also good chemistry.
It isn't fragile or lofty.
It's practical — like breathing, like sunlight, like soup on a cold day.
We survive on it.

Of course, the opposite is true too.
When we're hungry, tired, or scared, compassion shrinks.

The brain goes into survival mode, and the rest of us follows.
We become short-tempered, guarded, a little less generous.
It's not because we're bad — it's because we're running low.

Maybe that's why kindness can feel harder when the world feels tight.
We're trying to be good on an empty tank.
And it helps to remember that we can't pour warmth from a cold cup.
Sometimes the first act of compassion is to rest, to eat, to breathe — to become steady enough to share again.

It means love isn't some unreachable virtue.
It's built in.
It just needs the right conditions to grow.
And when it does, it changes everything — not just our mood, but our health, our habits, even the way we see one another.

So when we reach out, when we care, when we forgive — we're not defying our nature.
We're remembering it.

Repairing the Wires
It's one thing to understand that we're wired for love.
It's another to realize how many of us had that wiring crossed, frayed, or broken along the way.

Most of us, somewhere in our story, learned to pull away — to protect, to pretend, to stay busy.
We built whole lives around not needing too much.

199

And yet, no matter how far we go, the heart keeps sending the same signal: *reach out.*

The beautiful part is that repair is possible.
We can learn warmth again.
We can learn to trust again.
It doesn't happen all at once, but kindness has this quiet power to rewire us — moment by moment, gesture by gesture.

Sometimes it starts with something small.
A friend who stays on the phone a little longer than they need to.
A neighbor who checks in.
A nurse who squeezes a hand and says, "You're doing fine."
Every one of those moments is a tiny repair.
And little by little, the heart believes again.

I've seen it with Darla and one of her relatives who had Alzheimer's. By the end, her loved one no longer remembered who Darla was — not her name, not their history — but when Darla took her hand, something deeper recognized her. They would sit like that for an hour or two, fingers intertwined, the restlessness easing into calm. Memory may have faded, but the comfort of touch did not. It was a quiet reminder that love, once known, never truly disappears; it lingers beneath thought, waiting to be felt again.

We don't have to fix the whole world to feel its goodness.
It begins with simple, human exchanges: patience offered, forgiveness accepted, laughter shared.

Every act of grace, however small, strengthens the circuits that cruelty once burned.

We spend so much of our lives trying to be strong — to stand tall and unshaken — when what we really need is to be held, to hold, and to know that the same current runs through us all.
That's what compassion does: it keeps the current alive.

We rediscover it by accident.
We apologize, we listen, we forgive — and something inside us clicks back into place.
It feels like a small thing, but that's how all healing begins: not in grand gestures, but in gentle ones.
Love works quietly, and that's what makes it powerful.

Maybe this is the part of the story Harlow couldn't measure — the recovery, the rewiring, the way warmth returns to those who once lived without it.
Maybe love, at its deepest, isn't something we find but something we repair together.

When we offer kindness, we become part of someone else's healing.
When we receive it, we let them become part of ours.
And slowly, connection becomes what it always was meant to be — not a gift from a few to the many, but a shared inheritance we keep passing back and forth.

The Moral Blueprint Beneath the Skin
We often talk about morality as something we rise up to — a goal, a discipline, a choice between good and bad.
But maybe it's closer than that.
Maybe goodness isn't something above us, but something

beneath us — built into the wiring, waiting to be remembered.

When we show compassion, the body softens, the breath steadies, the heart opens.
It's as if the whole system exhales in recognition: *Yes, this is how it's supposed to be.*
Kindness feels natural because it is.
It restores a rhythm that life too easily disrupts.

We are all of us born with the capacity to love.
What life does — through fear, loss, and disappointment — is make us forget.
But forgetting is not the same as losing.
Every time we listen instead of react, forgive instead of withdraw, help instead of harden — we remember.

And when we remember, something larger than us stirs.
Not divine command, not moral perfection — just the quiet truth that we belong to one another.
We've seen it in the experiments, in the stories, in the small mercies that carry us from day to day.
We are not machines learning compassion; we are compassion learning to be human.

That's what love really is — not an invention, but a restoration.
Each time we reach out, we rebuild the original design: connection, safety, care.
It's older than language, older than belief, and still flowing beneath our skin.

So as we move forward, maybe the question isn't how do we become better?
But how do we remember who we already are?

22. The Logic of Fairness

Fairness usually shows up about the same time we learn the word *mine*.
Ask two of us to share a cookie, and you'll see the whole history of ethics unfold in about thirty seconds.
First comes the grab, then the glare, then the sudden burst of diplomacy:
"You can have the bigger half—if I get the crumbs."
It's a philosophy with crumbs on it.

Somewhere between nap time and snack time, we invented justice.
Not the courtroom kind—the kind that ends with someone crossing their arms and saying, "That's not fair!"
And deep down, we know they're right.
Fairness isn't something we're taught; it's something we feel tug at us, like gravity pulling toward balance.

I once watched a teacher solve a snack-time crisis with ancient wisdom: "One cuts, the other chooses."
You could feel the tension.
The first child sliced the brownie with surgical care; the second held both halves up to the light like a jeweler appraising diamonds.
Then the room exhaled and laughed.
That small laugh—the shared sigh of relief—is the sound

of community forming.
For a moment, the world was even.

We laugh at those moments, but there's something tender beneath them.
Fairness is our first act of empathy, the first time we notice that our happiness is tied to someone else's portion.
That's why even now, as adults splitting bills and taking turns at the stoplight, that small child inside us still pipes up—*Hey, that's not fair!*
It's the most democratic voice we have.

And maybe we keep chasing fairness all our lives because we remember, somewhere deep down, what it felt like to hold the smaller half and wish the world were kinder.
Fairness is the bridge we start building in the sandbox—between wanting and sharing, between self and other.
And the miracle is that we never stop trying to cross it together.

Tit for Tat: The Math of Morality
There's an old playground rhyme that goes:

"My mother and your mother live across the street,
Tit for tat, that's where we meet."

Sounds like a skipping song, doesn't it?
But in its own way, that's civilization talking—people figuring out how to live across the street from one another without throwing rocks.

"Tit for Tat" turned out to be more than a chant.
In the 1980s, a scientist named Robert Axelrod invited the

world's best strategists to create computer programs that could cooperate or compete in a game called *The Prisoner's Dilemma.*

It was basically a tournament of politeness—with math.

Each program had a choice: cooperate or betray.
In every round, two programs met and competed to get the best score.
And wouldn't you know, the simplest strategy of all won the whole thing.
It was called *Tit for Tat.*
It began with cooperation, copied whatever the other did next, and forgave easily.

That's it.
Start kind, stand firm, and forgive fast.
Apparently, even algorithms do better when they play nice.

The beauty of it is in its rhythm.
It's justice as a dance: step forward, step back, return to the same beat.
Be fair, but not foolish; gentle, but not gullible.
And when someone plays rough, give them a chance to come back to the rhythm.

It's funny to think that one of the most successful moral lessons of the century came not from a saint, but from a spreadsheet.
But maybe that's fitting.
Fairness is both heart and logic—it's the emotional intelligence of math.

"Tit for Tat" isn't about revenge; it's about remembering.

It says, "I'll meet you halfway if you'll meet me there too."
And that's where civilization really lives—right in the
middle.

The Playground of the Mind

Fairness doesn't end when we grow up.
It just moves from the sandbox to the conference room,
the grocery line, and the internet comment section.
We're all still learning to share.

But if you want to see fairness in its purest form, just
visit any playground.
You'll see the full spectrum: generosity, jealousy,
diplomacy, and chaos.
Kids make rules faster than adults make excuses.
They can spend fifteen minutes inventing a game and the
next fifteen arguing who broke it.
And still—somehow—it works.
By the end, there's laughter again.

I once saw two little boys try to divide a single
popsicle.
One held the stick, the other held the wrapper, and each
was convinced they had the short end of the deal.
Their teacher stepped in with a smile and said, "How
about we freeze another one and share that too?"
Both nodded, crisis averted.
Fairness, it seems, grows best in warm hands and cool
heads.

Researchers tell us children would rather go without
than see unfairness rewarded.
They'll reject a bigger prize if it means someone else gets

more.
They won't call it principle, but it is.
We can feel it too—that deep tug when things are off-balance.
It's not logic. It's something older.

Maybe that's why we groan at the slow line or the friend who always forgets their share.
It's not that we're petty; it's that our sense of fairness is built in.
We want the scales level because imbalance feels lonely.

But here's the catch: our fairness, even as adults, has borders.
We're quick to defend our own circle—our family, our team, our side.
It's easy to be fair with the people who think like us.
It's harder with the ones who don't.

Growing up, it seems, isn't about losing fairness.
It's about expanding it.
The moral test is whether we can keep the same fairness we learned in the sandbox when the world around us gets bigger and louder.

Growing the Circle
That widening of fairness—the stretch from "mine" to "ours"—is one of the great challenges of being human.
Peter Singer called it the "expanding circle."
Every time we include someone who was once outside our sympathy, we grow the moral world a little wider.

And sometimes, stories help us see it more clearly than theories ever could.

There's an old *Star Trek* episode called *"Arena."*
Captain Kirk finds himself stranded on a rocky planet,
forced to fight a lizard-like alien called the Gorn.
Each is armed with nothing but instinct and desperation.
Kirk, injured and furious, finally gains the upper hand.
He could kill his opponent—but he doesn't.
He sees the creature trembling, afraid, and lowers the
weapon.
"Maybe he thought he was defending himself," Kirk says
quietly.
And just like that, the alien stops being a monster and
becomes something closer to kin.

That's fairness growing up.
It's what happens when we realize that the "other side"
has a story too.
It's when our sense of justice shifts from *I deserve better* to
they deserve better, too.

We've been here before, across centuries and cultures.
The Good Samaritan stopped for a stranger.
A soldier shared bread with his enemy on Christmas Eve.
A teacher stood up for a student everyone else ignored.
Every moral breakthrough in history is fairness widening
its circle.

And every time we do it—every time we look at
someone we once feared or judged and say, *You belong
too*—the world takes one small step closer to balance.

When Fairness Turns Cold

Of course, fairness can turn on us, too.
Without compassion, it can become rigid, mathematical,

even cruel.

We've all seen what happens when rules outweigh mercy—when someone insists on being "technically right" while missing the human cost.

Modern life gives us endless examples: online mobs demanding perfect justice, systems that punish mistakes but never reward forgiveness.

We can be so determined to make the scales even that we forget who's on them.

Fairness without love becomes arithmetic.

Real justice needs warmth.

It needs someone willing to say, "You were wrong, but you're still one of us."

It needs the humility to admit that we've all had our unfair turns—on both sides of the scale.

When we lose that, fairness becomes cold metal instead of warm balance.

It starts counting instead of caring.

And that's when we have to remember what we learned back in the sandbox: the goal was never perfection.

It was sharing.

The Wisdom of Enough

At some point in life, we stop measuring halves and start measuring hearts.

We realize that fairness isn't about getting the same—it's about making sure everyone has *enough*.

That old trick of childhood fairness that still works: "You cut, I choose."

It teaches more than division—it teaches us trust.

We learn that fairness isn't enforced; it's *chosen*.
It's a kind of faith in one another.

Society depends on that trust. Every day, countless small, unseen acts of fairness prevent the world from falling apart.
We take turns in line, leave tips, hold doors open, and even share umbrellas.
We do these not because we are forced to, but because deep down we know: if it's fair for one, it's fair for all.

Fairness is love with a ruler—but a flexible one.
It bends toward kindness.
It remembers that being right isn't always the same as being good.

Maybe that's what justice was meant to be all along— not punishment, not perfection, but *balance.*
The steady back-and-forth that says, *Your share matters as much as mine.*
Tit for tat, that's where we meet.

And maybe we've been playing that game all our lives—learning, forgetting, forgiving, and starting over. That's the real rhythm of fairness: not getting even, but getting together.

23. The Hunger Beneath Behavior

The road is quiet again. That kind of quiet only comes
after a long rain—clean, muted, forgiving.
The tires whistle over damp asphalt, and the world smells
like soil and new beginnings.

We've come a long way.
We've talked about fairness, forgiveness, compassion—all
those big, shining words that sound like they belong to
the mind.
But the truth is, most of our moral lives happen long
before thought shows up.
Before philosophy, there's pulse.
Before empathy, there's energy—or the lack of it.

I sometimes laugh at how noble we think we are
before coffee.
Give us an empty stomach or a bad night's sleep, and
even saints start snapping.
For all our philosophy, we're still creatures of blood sugar
and breath.
The spirit may be willing, but the stomach gets the first
vote.

Robert Sapolsky once said, "We are not rational
creatures; we are rationalizing apes."
That line stings because it's true.
We like to imagine we decide with reason, but half the

time reason is just running behind with a clipboard saying, *"Yes, that's exactly what we meant to do."*

And maybe that's not such a terrible thing. Maybe it's humbling to realize that morality isn't something floating above our heads like a halo. It's something built from what we are: neurons, hormones, hunger, fear, fatigue.
We are both the clay and the hands shaping it.

So, as the road unwinds and the day begins, let's look closer at that hunger beneath behavior—not to excuse ourselves, but to understand how much effort goodness really takes when the body is tired, the heart is low, and the world keeps pressing for one more choice.

The Biology of a Choice
It usually starts small.
A friend says something sharp before breakfast, and suddenly the air between us thickens.
Then, an hour later—after coffee, after food—the apology: "Sorry, I was just hungry."
We laugh it off, but hunger has already revealed a truth philosophers rarely mention: virtue runs on calories.

Judges give longer sentences right before lunch.
Negotiators grow rigid when tired.
We've all barked at someone we love, then blamed it on the day, the drive, the growl in the stomach.
And maybe that's not just an excuse.
Maybe it's biology whispering through behavior.

Sapolsky reminds us that stress hormones, blood sugar, and even a passing cold can tip the scales between

patience and cruelty.
We like to picture ethics as marble—solid, unchanging—
but it's really more like water, constantly stirred by the
body that holds it.

Maybe the question isn't *why* people act badly, but
how rarely we act badly when we could.
Think about that for a second.
All the small kindnesses that happen every day despite
traffic, bills, aches, and fatigue—that's grace hiding in
biology's rough draft.

I remember once watching my father fix a neighbor's
fence on an empty stomach.
He hadn't eaten all day; Mom was cooking, slow and
steady.
When I asked why he didn't wait until after dinner, he
said, "Because it's leaning now."
He smiled, drove the nail straight, then said, "A man can
be hungry, but he shouldn't let his hunger make others
wait."
It was half proverb, half biology lesson.

Maybe morality is that simple—and that hard.
It's what we do before the meal, not after.

The Rationalizing Ape

We like to think reason leads the parade, but
neuroscience says otherwise.
Our feelings start the music; logic just catches up with a
baton.

Sapolsky jokes that our brains are "press secretaries
for our emotions."

We do something, then hold a little press conference in our heads explaining why it was noble, necessary, or at least *not our fault.*
It's not malice—it's wiring.

We build stories faster than we build fences.
We say, *"I didn't yell because I was angry; I yelled because someone needed to hear the truth."*
Or, *"I didn't honk because I'm impatient; I honked because the light was green."*
Each sentence is a small defense of identity: we want to stay the heroes of our own stories.

But honesty, the hard kind, begins when we pause long enough to see the ape behind the alibi.
We ask, "Was that really principle—or pride? Hunger—or hurt?"

We don't need shame to grow; we need curiosity.
And maybe laughter too.
Because once we see how messy and reactive we are, it's either laugh or despair.
I prefer laughter.
It keeps the humility gentle.

So yes, we are rationalizing apes—but we're also apes who can notice that, blush a little, and try again.
That's what makes us remarkable: self-awareness riding shotgun with self-deception, arguing over the map, and somehow still getting home.

The Thin Line of Control
There's a moment each day—sometimes at the grocery store, sometimes in traffic—when we meet that

thin line between choice and reflex.
The cart blocks the aisle; someone cuts in line; the world tests our patience.
And there it is again: biology, ready to vote first.

Psychologists call it *ego depletion*.
It sounds fancy, but it means our self-control tank runs dry.
The more we resist, the less we have left to resist with.
Kindness costs glucose.

That's why hungry children melt down faster, tired parents lose their temper sooner, and stressed workers snap at strangers.
The body is budgeting energy, not morality.

But here's the grace in it: once we understand this, we can build kindness into the system instead of expecting it to appear out of thin air.
Feed people before judgment.
Rest before decisions.
Pause before punishment.

My grandmother had a rule: *Never argue before dinner.*
She didn't need a Ph.D. in neuroscience; she had decades of living.
She knew that empty stomachs make sharp tongues.
So we ate first, argued later, and half the time the argument dissolved somewhere between the tortillas and the laughter.

Maybe compassion is just wisdom disguised as timing.
We're all better people when we've had a meal, a nap, or a little grace.

The Humility of Being Human

If Chapter 21 was about fairness, this one is about forgiveness — the forgiveness we owe ourselves for being built from such restless matter.
We are chemical creatures pretending to be angels, and somehow the pretending makes us kinder.

Understanding our biology doesn't excuse cruelty; it contextualizes it.
It reminds us that patience is an achievement, not a default.
Every gentle act is a small rebellion against evolution's impatience.

We like to think civilization sits atop nature, but really it floats within it.
Every law, every kindness, every moral code is a way of steering the old animal toward something gentler.

And there's beauty in that struggle.
When we hold the door despite irritation, when we swallow the angry word, when we forgive the tired friend — that's biology and compassion learning to waltz instead of wrestle.

Maybe morality isn't proof that we've escaped our nature, but that we've learned to listen to it — to its needs, its limits, its quiet pleas for rest.
We are miracle machines: half animal, half prayer.
And both sides deserve care.

So next time we feel that edge of impatience rising, maybe we just whisper to ourselves, "Eat something. Breathe. Then be kind."
Sometimes holiness is as simple as a sandwich.

Roots of Goodness

We began this chapter on the road, talking about hunger — the slight growl beneath behavior.
We end with gratitude for the simple truth that morality doesn't hover above the body; it grows inside it.

We've learned that our tempers follow our blood sugar, that our fairness follows our fatigue, that our compassion follows our chemistry.
But far from making us mechanical, that makes us marvelous.
Because, despite every hormone, hunger, and habit tugging at us, we still choose love more often than not.

If fairness were balance of the heart, this is balance of the flesh — learning to be gentle even when tired, patient even when hungry, forgiving even when flooded with noise and need.

Maybe goodness isn't the triumph of spirit over body. Maybe it's the friendship between them.
The spirit saying, *"I understand you're hungry,"* and the body answering, *"I'll try to be kind anyway."*

And that, in its humble way, is the real miracle of being human:
That compassion lives not in spite of what we are, but because of it.

24. The Theater of Distraction

The road bends toward home, golden in the last light.
We can already feel the evening waiting for us — a couch,
a soft chair, maybe the TV humming in the corner like a
friendly old dog.
We start wondering what we'll watch, what will fill the
space between dinner and sleep.
A little news, a little noise.
Something to make the day fade.

And maybe that's fair.
We've been thinking hard for a long time.
Sometimes we *want* to be distracted.
There's a strange mercy in turning down the volume of
our own thoughts.
Even John Lennon, after a life of noise, sang that he was
"just sitting here watching the wheels go round and
round."
That was his kind of peace — not escape, not
enlightenment, just breathing without ambition.
We can understand that.
Sometimes the mind needs rest the way the body needs
food.
But still — there's a difference between resting and
disappearing.

The streetlights come on.
Each one flickers awake like a thought we don't want to
have.
Every window we pass glows blue.
Every glow asks for attention.

The Economy of Attention

We live in an age that sells focus by the second.
Every swipe is an invitation: *Care about this. A recipe video
beside a war headline, a joke between two griefs — the feed
blends joy and horror until neither feels real.*
Every headline whispers: *You can't look away.*
We scroll and scroll, promising ourselves we'll stop after
the next one, the next, the next.
Then the soup burns, or the coffee cools, and we realize
an hour has slipped away.

It's not that we're lazy.
It's that the world has learned how to play us like a slot
machine — little rewards for little glances.
Each click is a coin.
Each headline is a lever.
The jackpot is our attention, and everyone's playing for it.

But attention isn't just mental energy; it's moral
currency.
What we look at shapes what we feel responsible for.
And when our eyes scatter, so does our compassion.
It's hard to love what you never linger on.

Still, we shouldn't scold ourselves too much.
Part of the reason we chase distractions is that we're
saturated.

We've seen too many tragedies, too many pleas, too many calls to care.
Our empathy gets sore.
So we hide in noise — not because we don't care, but because caring hurts.

The Outrage Loop

You've probably seen it — the daily parade of anger.
A scandal at breakfast, an argument by lunch, a new hero or villain by dinner.
It's the same show every day with a different cast.
We tell ourselves it's civic engagement, but most of the time it's theatre.
We watch outrage the way our ancestors watched gladiators.

Every headline says *look at this,* but few say *stay.*
We lurch from one heartbreak to another, too dizzy to help anyone.
It's not cruelty that drains our compassion; it's the pace.

I once overheard a couple arguing online — not in person, of course, but side-by-side on the couch, each defending humanity on their phones while ignoring the other's sighs.
I wanted to laugh, but I also recognized myself.
We argue about saving the world while the soup gets cold.

Sometimes we need to ask ourselves: *Are we participating, or just performing?*
The difference is quiet — almost invisible — but our hearts can feel it.

The Shadow on the Wall

There's a song by John Lennon where he says he's
"just sitting here watching shadows on the wall."
It sounds almost lazy — a man letting the world turn
without him.
But it reminds me of something much older: *Plato's
Allegory of the Cave.*

Imagine a group of people chained inside a cave since
birth.
Behind them burns a fire; before them, a wall.
Between the fire and the wall walk figures carrying objects
whose shadows dance in front of the prisoners.
The captives believe the shadows *are* the world.
Then one breaks free, steps outside, and is blinded by
sunlight — the real world so bright it hurts.
When he returns to tell the others, they laugh.
They'd rather keep their shadows.

Now, here we are — not in chains, but maybe in
habits.
We watch shadows of people on screens, shadows of truth
in headlines, shadows of love in likes and hearts.
We call them real because they're familiar.
And yet, like Lennon, part of us whispers, *I don't really
want to know.*
Maybe it's safer to watch than to wake.
Reality asks too much.
It asks us to act.

What a strange pair they make, Plato and Lennon —
one saying, *step out into the light,* the other saying, *I'm fine
right here.*
And perhaps both are right, depending on the day.

Sometimes we need the sun; sometimes we need the shade.

The Comfort of Noise

There's comfort in the flicker of a screen, the low hum of the television, the illusion that the world is still turning even when we're still.
We tell ourselves we'll watch for a few minutes, just to unwind — and that's fine.
But somewhere between resting and forgetting, the line blurs.

Maybe that's why quiet feels so awkward now.
We reach for the phone the way we used to reach for prayer beads — something to hold the moment still.
But stillness isn't what we fear; it's what might surface in it.
Old thoughts. Old guilt. Unanswered kindnesses.
The mind starts whispering the things the noise had been keeping down.

Sometimes distraction isn't the enemy of morality.
Sometimes it's anesthesia for the ache of caring.
We all need a little of it — a favorite show, a song, a late-night scroll.
The trick is remembering to come back.

Learning to Linger

Presence has become a radical act.
In a world of flashes and feeds, choosing to stay — to truly notice — feels almost rebellious.
Maybe that's what compassion is at its core: a willingness

to linger.
To look without flinching, to listen without multitasking.

I think of a time Darla and I were having dinner.
The power went out halfway through the meal.
No phones, no music, just candlelight and the sound of
rain on the roof.
We started laughing at first — two people marooned with
their own conversation.
But then, slowly, we remembered how good it feels to
really talk.
We stayed long after the lights came back, pretending
they hadn't.
I don't remember what I ate that night, but I remember
the glow on her face when she said, "I'd forgotten how
quiet feels."
We all forget.

So maybe that's the small work of this chapter — to
remember.
To pause the play, mute the feed, and sit with the
shadows long enough to see what they're hiding.
If we can do that, even for a few minutes a day, the world
starts to breathe again.

Attention as Compassion
We started this ride home dreaming of distractions,
and maybe that's okay.
The mind, like the body, needs rest.
But now we've seen how easily rest turns into retreat.
The danger isn't in watching the shadows; it's in
forgetting that they're shadows.

Distraction is the new distance.
It doesn't stretch miles between us; it slips seconds
between moments of noticing.
And yet, every act of focus — every moment we look fully
at someone, or something, and stay — is a small rebellion
against the cave.

Maybe we can learn to use distraction kindly: watch a
film that makes us laugh, a song that lets us feel, a story
that reminds us we're not alone.
But let's not mistake comfort for connection.
When the screen goes dark, let's linger a little longer with
the world still glowing outside it.

*"Love, after all, begins — and stays — where attention
does."*

And maybe, as Lennon sang, we don't always want to
know everything — but we can still *notice* what's real,
quietly, together, as the wheels keep turning and the road
leads home.

25. The Crowd at the Gallows

The road narrows as the sun sinks.
There's a stillness to the air, the kind that comes before a
hush — or a shout.
We're heading home, or at least we thought we were,
when we notice people standing ahead, shoulders close,
faces turned toward something unseen.
We can't yet tell what draws them, only that they're
drawn.

Crowds have a kind of gravity. Maybe that's why
crowds feel holy and dangerous at once — we sense a
power larger than any one of us, and it tempts us to stop
thinking for ourselves.
They pull more than bodies — they pull judgment.
Part of us wants to stay clear, another part wants to know.
It's a small, familiar tug: *What's everyone looking at?*
That question has followed humankind longer than any
map or border.

Long ago, crowds gathered in the square when the
church bell rang or the drums began.
They came for weddings, for speeches, for justice — or
what passed for it.
Sometimes it was for a hanging.
They said it was to keep order, to remind the town what

happens to thieves or traitors.
But there's another truth underneath: people came to *see*.

Even as children, we understood that pull.
I remember a teacher telling my classmates and me—
almost casually—that during a time when public
hangings were common, pickpockets would blend into
the crowd, stealing from people while others looked on,
watching a man swinging for doing the very same things
they did. The irony was clear and sharp, even to a child. It
wasn't just that the gallows didn't prevent crime; more
striking was the laughter that presumably echoed around
such scenes. The thought that anyone could smile while
another person's life was ending seemed impossible. Yet,
history shows that they did.

We like to think we're better now.
We have laws, courts, cameras, and commentators.
But the instinct that gathers a crowd hasn't changed
much.
It's older than any civilization — that strange mixture of
fear, curiosity, and belonging.
We want to be near the heat, even if it burns.

The question that stays with us isn't about *them* — the
ones in the crowd.
It's about *us*.
If we had lived then — if we'd heard the bell, seen the
people moving down the street — would we have gone
too?
Would we have stood at the edge, telling ourselves we
were only watching?

The light fades, and the voices ahead blur into a low hum.
Whatever they're gathered for, it isn't joy.
But still, it draws us forward — as if knowing were safer than wondering.
And that, perhaps, is where every crowd begins.

The Smiling Crowd

Once, years later, I saw a photograph on the internet.
It was an old image — early 1900s, I think — of a lynching.
You've probably seen one like it.
Not just the victim, but the *crowd*: men and women in their Sunday best, smiling, pointing, children perched on shoulders.
They looked as if they'd come from a picnic.

That photo unsettled me more than almost anything I've ever seen.
It wasn't the violence that hollowed me out — it was the joy.
Ordinary people, grinning, frozen in time beside death as if posing with a celebrity.
The darkness wasn't in what they'd done, but in how *familiar* they looked.
People like us.

I remember staring at that photo for a long time.
My stomach turned, but my eyes wouldn't look away.
And I thought of Sapolsky's line: *we are not rational creatures; we are rationalizing apes.*
Raised in another time, another place, might I have been there too, telling myself I was upholding order, protecting

228

decency, doing what everyone else was doing?

It's easy to say no.

But history is full of people who thought the same thing about their own age.

We like to focus on the bright side of evolution — the part that gave us community and cooperation.

But we forget that the same instincts that make us social also make us cruel in groups.

The same urge that binds us together can blind us, too.

That photo isn't just a record of hate.

It's a mirror — one that asks, "If the crowd cheers, will you?"

The Colosseum

The Romans understood the crowd better than anyone.

They built their cities around it.

In the Colosseum, fifty thousand people could gather to watch men die for sport, animals tear each other apart, blood soaking the sand.

It wasn't an aberration — it was entertainment.

A ticketed event, with vendors, music, and applause.

The emperors called it *panem et circenses* — bread and circuses.

Feed the people, entertain them, and they won't ask for justice.

We haven't built stone arenas in a while, but the impulse lingers.

We gather for football, for fights, for reality shows that humiliate strangers, for viral videos that turn pain into

spectacle.
The Colosseum lives in every stadium and every comment thread where we cheer someone's downfall.
We pretend it's different because we sell popcorn instead of punishment, but the crowd's appetite hasn't changed.

I've heard people say they go to car races for the speed, the skill, the engineering.
But when the engines roar, and the cars spin out, everyone stands up.
No one wants anyone hurt — not really — but the pulse quickens just the same.
There's something in us that leans toward danger, that wants to see what happens next.
That's not evil.
It's curiosity mixed with adrenaline, the same reflex that once helped us survive in the wild.
We watch because we can't not watch.

The trouble is, once you start watching suffering long enough, it stops looking like suffering.
It becomes *content*.
And when pain turns into entertainment, compassion becomes background noise.

The Mirror of Evolution

Robert Sapolsky once said that our brains are like old cathedrals: we've built new rooms for reason, but the foundation is still animal.
Inside us lives the same machinery that once kept our ancestors alive in the savanna — the fight-or-flight reflex, the mob instinct, the thrill of dominance.
Most days, it stays quietly beneath our manners.

But give it a crowd, a leader, a target — and the old brain wakes up.

It's not that we're monsters.
We're just built for survival, not sanctity.
Morality is the upgrade — the software written over the animal code.
But it's fragile.
It flickers when fear rises or when belonging feels threatened.

So much of who we are is determined by the tribe that names right and wrong for us.
In a different century, we might have believed different things with the same conviction we hold now.
That doesn't excuse cruelty, but it explains its reach.
We aren't born moral; we learn morality the way we learn language — by hearing it spoken around us.

And that's what makes forgiveness, courage, and compassion such miracles: they aren't instincts.
They're rebellions against instinct.
They're the moments when the cathedral walls hold, when the new brain says no to the old one.

Would I Go?

Sometimes I try to imagine it. If I lived in Rome, would I have gone to the Colosseum?
If I lived in the South a hundred years ago, would I have stood in that crowd?
If I lived in Salem, would I have shouted for the witch to burn?
It's easy to say no — we all say no.

But morality isn't proved by our answers; it's revealed by our discomfort.

Maybe the better question is: *why do I want to believe I wouldn't?*
What fear am I protecting?
What comfort am I clinging to?

We're quick to condemn the past because it's safe to do so.
But the point of looking back isn't to prove our superiority — it's to see our reflection.
Every time we slow down to stare at a wreck on the highway, some part of that ancient crowd still lives in us.
We lean toward the noise because silence asks more of us.

Sapolsky reminds us: we're not rational, just rationalizing.
And maybe that's why it matters to pause and ask — not to wallow in guilt, but to remember that goodness takes work.
We inherit instincts; we *build* compassion.

The Courage of Stillness
The bravest souls in history are often the quietest ones.
They don't hold signs or lead chants.
They stand still when others cheer.
They look away when looking would make them complicit.
They reach down when the crowd steps back.

Every generation builds its own Colosseum — some made of stone, some made of screens.

Each time, a few souls choose silence over spectacle.
Those are the ones who keep the world from slipping too far.

It takes courage to speak, yes.
But sometimes it takes more to refuse to join the roar.
To say nothing, to walk away, to let empathy outweigh curiosity.
Kindness rarely gets applause — and that's how you know it's real.

The Empty Square

Eventually, the crowd thins.
The voices scatter, the square empties, and what felt like an event fades into ordinary air.
The silence that follows always feels strange — heavier somehow.
Maybe it's the echo of our own thoughts.

Every spectacle ends.
Every crowd dissolves.
What remains is how we behaved while it burned.
We can't change what our ancestors cheered for, but we can decide what we'll clap for now.

The world has its noise, shows, and battles.
We'll still slow down for a wreck sometimes — curiosity isn't a sin, just human nature. But maybe we can learn to notice when the line between observing and participating begins to blur.
That's the moment when conscience whispers, Enough.
And maybe that's where goodness begins:

In the moment we stop to ask,
Would I have gone?

26. The Moral Landscape Revisited

The road widens after the square.
We ride quietly for a while, the tires whispering over the
pavement, the air cooler now that evening has taken hold.
It feels like the world itself is sighing.
After so much noise and judgment, even the wind feels
like forgiveness.

No one talks at first.
We're still shaking off the weight of what we saw — not a
scene, really, but a question: *Would I have gone?*
It lingers, but the farther we ride, the more distance
softens it.
Ahead, the hills open into long stretches of gold and
green.
A dog barks somewhere, a child laughs, and suddenly the
world feels innocent again.

"Let's stop for ice cream," someone says.
We all laugh because, of course, that's exactly what the
moment needs.
A little sweetness after the bitter.
There's something healing about the ordinary — the
drone of a freezer, the scoop hitting the cone, the first cold
taste after a long day of thinking.

Maybe that's how moral recovery works, too — one
small kindness after a hard look at cruelty.

We rebuild the soul the same way we rebuild trust: in small scoops.

The View from the Hill

We find a long hill that overlooks the valley, and we stop halfway up, catching our breath.
From here, the world looks patient.

If compassion had geography, it might look like this.

Sam Harris once described morality as a kind of landscape — peaks of well-being, valleys of suffering — and the work of our lives is simply to keep climbing together. It's a helpful image, because once we start seeing goodness as movement rather than perfection, we notice how often we're already inching upward.

And the climb isn't just metaphorical.
Others have tried to measure it.

Steven Pinker, for example, points out that over centuries, violence has fallen, rights have expanded, and — despite how it feels on any given news day — the long arc has been bending toward less suffering, not more.

We'd never guess it from watching the headlines.
If we believed every broadcast, we'd think the sky was collapsing daily.

But the sky, so far, keeps holding.

Maybe that's because goodness rarely announces itself.
Progress whispers.
It does its work in hospitals and classrooms, in kitchens

236

and shelters, in all the places where people tend to one another quietly.

Civilizations don't usually fall off cliffs.
They rise and slip and rise again, like this hill beneath our feet — and most of us, in ways small and steady, are still pushing upward.

The Fellow Travelers

As we start rolling again, we pass people — a farmer checking a gate, a nurse walking home, a teenager waving from a porch.
Ordinary scenes that mean everything when you look closely.

For every act of cruelty we've ever studied, there are a thousand quiet acts of decency that no one records.
The man who pulls over to help change a tire.
The neighbor who shovels two driveways instead of one.
The nurse who stays after her shift because the patient looks lonely.
They won't make history, but they make the world livable.

We laugh when we think of how dramatic we get about "the end of humanity."
Humanity, bless it, has been ending for thousands of years and still manages to show up for work on Monday.
Civilization never fell — it just stopped posting about its wins.

Moral progress is slower than we want it to be, but it's happening.
Most of the time, it rides a bike, not a rocket.

The Detour Sign

Not far from town, a big orange DETOUR sign points us down a side road.

We groan, but take it anyway.

The road curves through a small grove of trees, rough and narrow.

It smells of earth and rain.

The kind of road you don't plan on but end up glad you found.

Moral progress looks a lot like this, doesn't it?

We pave, we patch, we get lost, we circle back.

We set up signs for the next traveler and hope they hold.

Every generation leaves a map drawn in pencil.

I think about times I've taken the wrong road and stumbled into beauty.

A diner in the middle of nowhere, a song playing on the jukebox, the kind of conversation that lasts longer than the coffee.

Maybe morality works that way — we don't always know where the good road is until we've missed it once or twice.

We complain about the potholes, but forget how far we've paved.

The Conversation on the Ride

The detour winds us back toward home, and as the sky deepens to a slow lavender, someone says, "Do you realize how much ground we've covered?"

We laugh because we know they don't just mean the miles.

We've crossed love, compassion, forgiveness, fear, hunger, cruelty, distraction — the whole human map. If philosophy were measured in mileage, we'd need new tires.

But every mile has mattered. Each turn has shown us that, given the chance, most people try to be good. We fail, of course — often, spectacularly. But we learn, too. Slowly. Stubbornly. Beautifully.

There's a kind of joy in that, isn't there? Knowing that even when we stumble, we still keep building a world that's a little gentler than the one before it.

The Road Home

At last, we crest the final hill, and there it is — home. A warm porch light glowing through the dusk, the faint smell of supper drifting through the air. The ride feels longer now, but the kind of long that means something. Our legs are tired, but our spirits aren't.

Maybe morality isn't about perfection. Maybe it's about persistence — the choice to keep pedaling toward the light, no matter how many wrong turns we've taken. The world may still be messy, but it's ours to keep mending.

One act of kindness, one honest word, one slow, steady mile at a time.

We lean our bikes against the porch, look back once at the road, and smile.
It's not a bad landscape after all.
Not perfect.
Just better than yesterday.
And maybe that's the best view any of us can hope for.

27. Every Road Leads Home

The porch light glows like an old friend.
The air smells like rain and dust and something warm —
maybe someone's cooking down the street.
We lean our bikes against the railing and just stand there
for a moment, letting the quiet settle in.

We've been out for a long time, haven't we?
A whole journey — through love, cruelty, forgiveness,
fairness, hunger, and hope.
And now… we're home.

The stillness feels strange at first.
After so many words, the silence feels like an echo.
But then again, silence is just the sound of a full day
catching its breath.

We step inside, kick off our shoes, and feel the cool
floor under our feet.
The sound of the refrigerator, the creak of the chair — it's
the music of ordinary life.
And maybe that's what we were looking for all along.

The TV Comes On
Out of habit, we reach for the remote.
Click.

The screen blinks to life — a talk show, a headline, another tragedy far away.
Somewhere, people are crying. Somewhere else, people are arguing about who's to blame.

We stand there, staring, holding the remote like a moral compass that's lost its needle.

It's strange how compassion can fade the farther it travels.
We ache for the people next door, but the ones across the ocean feel like shadows.

Peter Singer tried to warn us about that — how a child drowning close by shakes us more than a thousand hungry children that are miles away.
He wasn't scolding us; he was reminding us that empathy is a muscle.
It weakens when we stop using it.

We tell ourselves we should care more.
But we also know that caring isn't a button we press — it's a habit we practice.
Sometimes we just need to look a little longer before turning the channel.

We sigh and smile a little.
"It's hard to save the world," we say to no one in particular, "when we can't even find the remote."

The Hunger Beneath It
Our stomach growls.
We laugh — apparently philosophy burns calories.

So we head to the kitchen and put together something
simple — eggs, maybe soup.
The kind of meal that doesn't judge us.

Sapolsky would say hunger narrows the moral lens
— that when the stomach's empty, the brain turns tribal.
We feel that truth every time we cook.
The world gets smaller — it becomes about heat, timing,
salt, smell.

And yet somehow, that smallness grounds us.
It reminds us that morality isn't built in lecture halls; it's
built around tables.

We stir the pot and think:
Maybe we overcomplicate goodness.
Maybe it's not grand speeches or perfect systems.
Maybe it's feeding whoever's hungry — even if it's just
ourselves.

We tell ourselves it's mindfulness, but it's probably
just dinner.
Still, it's something.

The Argument on the Screen
We wander back with our bowl, and the TV has
switched to the news.
Now it's a debate — red faces, raised voices, everyone so
sure of themselves.

They're talking about justice and fairness as if
shouting loudly enough makes one of them right.

It's strange — everyone wants to win, but no one
wants to understand.

We think about what we said earlier in this book:
Seek to understand before being understood.

It's easy to forget that when there's a microphone involved.

Justice, mercy, forgiveness — they're not enemies.
They're neighbors who keep slamming each other's doors.

And the world listens more to the shouting than to the silence that follows.

We remember those people we talked about — the ones who forgave unthinkable things.
The Charleston churchgoers who prayed with a man before he killed them, then forgave him anyway.
The bombing victim who let go of rage because it was too heavy to carry.

They didn't win debates.
They healed wounds.

The Commercial Break
The screen cuts to a smiling family selling laundry detergent.
It's such a clean pivot from tragedy to tidiness that we almost laugh.

We've traded the gallows for the commercial.
Distraction doesn't look violent anymore; it just looks... pleasant.

But we've learned a few things about attention.
If love begins where we linger, then every ad break is a moral test.

Do we stay awake to what matters, or drift toward what's easy?

We pick up the remote again and press mute.

The silence returns, soft and kind.
Sometimes love is just muting the noise long enough to hear our own heart again.

The Dinner Table

We sit at the table, the soup steaming in front of us.
It's simple — a mix of what's left in the fridge.
Still, it tastes like effort, and effort tastes good.

We think about Ubuntu — *I am because we are.*
About fairness, forgiveness, and that long road we've traveled.

All of it leads back here — the table, the meal, the warmth of being alive together.
Most goodness starts like this: small, shared, unseen.

We remember saying once that fairness is love with a ruler — but a flexible one.
Maybe that's what we're tasting now: flexible love.
Not perfect, but nourishing.

The Window

After dinner, we stand by the window and look out.
The glass reflects us faintly — the same people, maybe a little wiser, a little humbler.

We think of that awful photo — a crowd posing in front of a body, smiling.
We've seen how far indifference can go.

But we've also seen what happens when a few refuse to follow the crowd.
Farmers who hid families.
Nurses who smuggled medicine.
Strangers who said, "Not this time."

Even in our darkest moments, someone always whispers,
This isn't right.

And maybe that's the best thing we've learned:
Goodness never disappears; it just waits for courage to find it.

We don't know what we would've done, had we lived then.
But we hope, at least now, we'd have second thoughts — and that might be enough to change everything.

The Quiet Room
We turn off the TV. The buzzing stops.
The room feels heavy, but peaceful — like an exhale that's been waiting all day.

The shadows move across the wall, but they're not convincing anymore.

We think of John Lennon's line:
"I'm just sitting here watching the wheels go round and round."

Maybe he wasn't bored — maybe he'd finally stopped chasing shadows.

We don't need to chase meaning forever.
Sometimes it finds us when we sit still long enough.

We've seen cruelty and beauty, hunger and grace, fear and forgiveness — and we're still here.
That counts for something.

That's the quiet triumph of being human: we keep trying.

The Porch Light

We step outside one last time.
The night air is cool and full of cricket song.
The bikes lean against the porch where we left them, muddy but faithful.

The street is quiet.
Home smells like the world made small again.

We've seen so much — love, cruelty, compassion, exhaustion.
We've wrestled with gods and apes, saints and scientists, all trying to say the same thing:

Care. Just care.

Mother Teresa once said, "Love begins at home."
Maybe that's why every road, no matter how far it winds, leads back to the same front door.

Love starts in the places we know — our kitchens, our arguments, our quiet evenings.
Then, if we're lucky, it grows into something that touches the neighbor, the stranger, and maybe, someday, the world.

We turn off the porch light, step inside, and close the door behind us.
The house hums softly — a steady, living heartbeat.

And in that quiet, simple room, we realize:

We are home.

Before We Go

If you've made it this far, thank you for walking — or riding — beside me.
We've traveled through some rough weather together: love and loss, fear and forgiveness, cruelty and courage.
We've met philosophers, scientists, strangers, and saints.
We've looked hard at the darkness and then, somehow, found light.

But this was never really a book about ideas.
It was about people.
About us.
About the small, stubborn hope that goodness still matters — and that we can practice it, even when the world feels too loud or too far gone.

I don't pretend to have the answers.
Some days, I don't even know the right questions.
But I do know that kindness never wastes its time, and that gentleness has never once made the world worse.

So wherever this finds you — in a busy kitchen, or a quiet room, or sitting alone after a long day — remember:
You don't have to fix the whole world.
Just care for your corner of it.
One word, one act, one heartbeat at a time.

And if you forget, that's alright too.
We'll remind each other.
Because love doesn't need to be perfect.
It just needs to begin — right where we are.

(pause... a soft smile)

Now, go home.
Turn on a light.
Call someone you love.
And if there's a little warmth left over
let it spill.

Acknowledgments & Inspirations

This book was never meant to preach — it was meant to listen.
To the quiet wisdom found in stories, in science, and in the people who taught me, often without knowing they were teaching.

I owe heartfelt thanks to those who helped me see love and compassion from many sides:
To **Leo Tolstoy**, for showing that moral clarity can live in the innocence of children;
to **Kahlil Gibran**, whose *Sand and Foam* taught that gentleness is its own kind of courage;
to **Mother Teresa**, who reminded us that love begins at home;
to **Peter Singer**, whose *Expanding Circle* opened the borders of empathy;
and to **Immanuel Kant**, who insisted that every person carries inherent worth.

To **Jean-Paul Sartre**, for showing that freedom is both burden and grace;
to **Hannah Arendt** and **Socrates**, who reminded us that morality begins in honest conversation;
to **Plato**, for the idea that wisdom is remembering what we already know;

251

And to **John Lewis**, for the quiet, enduring power of gentleness in action.

I'm grateful to the storytellers who turned ideas into life:
Jack London, for Otoo's brotherhood;
Lloyd Alexander, for the strength of humble heroes;
The tellers of **The Arabian Nights**, for proving that even the wildest stories can heal;
and **John Green**, for helping me see that memory, grief, and love are all different tenses of the same truth.

From the realm of science and thought:
Robert Sapolsky, for revealing the biology behind compassion and cruelty;
Steven Pinker, for reminding us that empathy, though fragile, has been rising for centuries;
Sam Harris, for daring to ground morality in reason and care;
Daniel Beyer, for exploring the luminous machinery of mind and consciousness;
Viktor Frankl, for showing that meaning can survive even in suffering;
Ralph Waldo Emerson, for urging us to be honest enough to change;
and **Friedrich Nietzsche**, for the hard lesson that even struggle can give birth to beauty.

I also owe quiet gratitude to the teachers of spirit and balance:
Buddha, for the stillness behind every storm;
Confucius, and **Mencius** and **Xunzi**, for the humanity within order and the argument about what goodness asks of us;

252

St. Paul and St. Luke, for shaping the early language of love;
Gandhi, for making compassion a practice;
Marcus Aurelius, for the calm strength of stoicism;
and Epictetus, for the simple truth that we may not control life, but we can always control our response.

From modern voices, I carry lessons from Daniel Kahneman and Jonathan Haidt, who mapped the moral mind;
Carl Rogers and Abraham Maslow, who saw human goodness as potential, not theory;
and from Nel Noddings, for showing that ethics begins in care, not command.
To Mark Sheskin, Paul Bloom, and Karen Wynn, who helped reveal that fairness and kindness are born early in us.
To Albert Camus, for reminding us that even in an absurd world, we can choose compassion.
And to the many unnamed thinkers, writers, and wanderers whose words have become part of mine.

But above all, my deepest gratitude is to Darla, whose love gave these pages their warmth;
to my parents, whose quiet lessons on kindness and humility formed the moral compass behind every story;
and to every reader who believes, even for a moment, that love and understanding can still make a difference.

Because they can.
And that's why this book exists.

www.ingramcontent.com/pod-product-compliance
Lightning Source LLC
Chambersburg PA
CBHW022048020426
42335CB00012B/590